THE
MILLENNIUM

Books by Father McBride

*The Kingdom and the Glory: Commentary on Matthew
*To Love and Be Loved by Jesus: Commentary on Mark
*The Human Face of Jesus: A Commentary on Luke
*The Divine Presence of Jesus: A Commentary on John
*The Gospel of the Holy Spirit: A Commentary on Acts
*The Second Coming of Jesus: A Commentary on
Apocalypse
*Essentials of the Faith
*Father McBride's Teen Catechism
*Father McBride's Family Catechism
*Millennium: End of Time? A New Beginning?
Invitation: A Catholic Learning Guide
The Seven Last Words of Jesus
A Retreat with Pope John XXIII
The Story of the Church
Catholic Evangelization
Images of Jesus
Images of Mary
Saints Are People

Other books by Father McBride

Homilies for the New Liturgy
Catechetics: A Theology of Proclamation
A Short Course on the Bible
The Human Dimensions of Catechetics
The Pearl and the Seed
Heschel: Religious Educator
Growing in Grace: Bible History
Christian Formation of Catholic Education
Year of the Lord: Cycles A,B,C
Father McBride's Homily Reflections: Cycles A,B,C
Death Shall Have No Dominion
Creative Teaching in Christian Education
The Quest For Content in Christian Education
Catechists Never Stop Learning
The Ten Commandments: Sounds of Love From Sinai
Staying Faithful

*Published by Our Sunday Visitor, Inc.

THE
MILLENNIUM
End of Time? A New Beginning?

Alfred McBride
O.Praem.

Our Sunday Visitor Publishing Division
Our Sunday Visitor, Inc.
Huntington, Indiana 46750

Our Sunday Visitor Publishing Division
Our Sunday Visitor, Inc.
200 Noll Plaza
Huntington, IN 46750

ISBN: 0-87973-685-2
LCCCN: 98-65869

Cover design by Rebecca Heaston
PRINTED IN THE UNITED STATES OF AMERICA
685

This book is dedicated to the students in my Book of Revelation Seminar at Pope John XXIII National Seminary, Weston, Massachusetts, for their creative and intelligent contribution to the study of the Second Coming of our Lord.

TABLE OF CONTENTS

PREFACE 9

PART ONE:
THE MILLENNIUM AS THE END OF TIME

CHAPTER ONE:
  SOUND THE ALARM! THE END IS COMING! 17
CHAPTER TWO:
  IS THE ANTICHRIST KNOCKING AT YOUR DOOR? 31
CHAPTER THREE:
  GET READY FOR THE RAPTURE 43
CHAPTER FOUR:
  HAVE DANIEL'S SEVENTY WEEKS
  OF YEARS ARRIVED? 55
CHAPTER FIVE:
  JOACHIM OF FIORE VS. AUGUSTINE AND EZEKIEL 67
CHAPTER SIX:
  WHOSE "FOUR LAST THINGS"
  SHOULD YOU BELIEVE? 81

PART TWO:
THE MILLENNIUM AS A JUBILEE

CHAPTER SEVEN:
  CELEBRATE A JUBILEE 97
CHAPTER EIGHT:
  O JESUS, JOY OF LOVING HEARTS 109
CHAPTER NINE:
  SANCTIFIED BY THE SPIRIT 121
CHAPTER TEN:
  GLORIFIED BY THE FATHER 135

INDEX 149

Preface

Who's Afraid of the Millennium?

Recently the New York Times featured a full page ad with the headlines: THE MILLENNIUM IS COMING! YOU WANT TO MAKE SOMETHING OF IT? These words were set against a global backdrop. The text continued: "December 31, 1999. A few determined souls have made their way to uninhabited Caroline Island, Kiribati, in the central Pacific Ocean. Their goal: to be the first people on earth to witness the dawning of the new millennium. At 15:43 Greenwich Mean Time the light lifts at the edge of the horizon. The watchers try not to blink."

The ad was sponsored by the Jewish Theological Seminary as a message to celebrate the High Holy Day. The remaining text of the ad pointed out the arbitrary character of the dating of the millennium. It also mentioned that the best way to celebrate the date is to give meaning to our own time by making our days holy. Examples: Ten years of love, despite everything. The hours when a jury struggles through to justice. The moment when a congregation stands in a silence pierced by the sound of the shofar. One year clean and sober. Observing the Sabbath.

The ad shows contrasting approaches to the millennium.

What is the millennium anyhow?

Is it a signal that the end of time is upon us as some millenarians would have us believe?

Or is it a Jubilee, a time to celebrate and renew the self, the Church, and the world as Pope John Paul II urges us?

In this book I have decided to reflect on the millennium in the light of each of these questions.

First I should assure my readers that I am aware of the

arbitrariness of using our year 2000 as the key date. Some properly say it should be 2001. Others point out that, as the date of Christ's 2,000th birthday, a more accurate date from a scholar's point of view would probably be 1996 — and so on. Nonetheless, I will use 2000 as our commonly accepted time for commemorating Christ's birth and the beginning of the Third Millennium.

In this book I confine my reflections to responding to the two questions mentioned above. Part One will deal with those who associate millennium with the end of time. Part Two will approach the millennium as a Jubilee.

In Part One I will try to explain the teachings of contemporary millenarians. What is their view of the antichrist? Why do they assign so much importance to what they call the rapture? How did they come to take prophecies in the Book of Daniel and apply them to geopolitical events today, especially the founding of the state of Israel in 1948? Who was Joachim of Fiore, and what would Augustine think of him had he known him?

I will compare the "four last things" of millenarians to those held by Catholics. I will show the millenarian method of interpreting Scripture and its unacceptability for Catholics. I will point out that the millenarian "postponement theory of history" is a gratuitous way of interpreting history and is without basis in fact. I will also make some reference to the variety of millenarian schools such as the pre- and post-dispensationalists.

I note that millenarians do take the Christian doctrine of the Second Coming seriously. It seems to give them their fervor, enthusiasm, and dynamism. Catholics believe in the Second Coming, confess it every Sunday in the Nicene Creed, and hear a Last Judgment Gospel every year on the thirty-third Sunday of Ordinary Time. But generally, Catholics do not derive much spiritual drive from the doctrine.

I believe that Catholics need the spiritual enthusiasm that Christ's Second Coming engenders. The New Testament shows that the first Christians were intensely interested in and motivated by the anticipated Second Coming of Jesus. The final verses of the New Testament leaves us with their shout of hope, "Maranatha! Come, Lord Jesus!" (Rev 22:20).

Millenarians, however, have something to learn from Catholics. They would benefit from Catholic reserve about naming the exact date of Christ's final arrival in glory. They would be better off imitating Catholic reticence about how the end times will occur, and therefore, not drawing literal applications from the prophecies of Daniel to our present geopolitical situation.

Christ's Second Coming is a divine mystery because the time and manner of this manifestation is reserved to the hidden plan of God. Our proper response is one of faith in the truth of the teaching — and a daily commitment to the Christian way of life regardless of when, exactly, Jesus will come in glory.

THE GREAT JUBILEE

Pope John Paul II has been interested in the Third Millennium since the beginning of his pontificate more than nineteen years ago. He has published a document about how this event should be celebrated, *Tertio Millennio Adveniente* ("The Coming Third Millennium"). John Paul considers the date as a time for a Great Jubilee celebrating the beginning of the Third Millennium of Christianity and a fresh start in proclaiming Jesus Christ and all he means for our salvation and the world.

Interestingly, he does not quote from Revelation 20:1-6, where the word millennium (or thousand-year reign) appears six times, and is the key text for millenarians. There is no doubt at all that the pope believes in the doctrine of the Second Coming, but he has chosen the biblical theme of Jubilee as the way to commemorate the year 2000 rather than a special focus on the Second Coming or the end of time.

Part Two of this book lays out the papal direction for how to celebrate a Great Jubilee in 2000. We should make it a resounding hymn of joy and praise for the gift of Jesus our Savior, the Spirit our Sanctifier, and the Father who wants to glorify us in eternal life. We should make the Jubilee a time of personal conversion and repentance for our sins. We ought to mark the new millennium with an enthusiastic re-commitment to ecumenism and interreligious dialogue.

Let it be a time for a new evangelization of nations, the revival of the ancient missionary spirit of the Church, sharing our faith with a contagious love of Christ, and an affection for those with whom we wish to open our hearts. Celebrate the Jubilee with a revitalized compassion for the poor of the world, a resolve to bring to every human being the justice and dignity they deserve, and an energetic support for an enduring peace for all peoples.

Adopt the attitude of Jesus who did not come to condemn the world but to save it (see John 3:17). Jesus knew all about the sins of the people with whom he dealt, such as the woman taken in adultery. Christ told her he would not condemn her, even as he urged her to sin no more. We will be far better advised to bring to every person the medicine of mercy so that we can offer them Christ's salvation from their sinfulness.

Pray constantly for the power of the Holy Spirit to make the call to holiness a reality for everyone. Meditate on John 16:8, which teaches us that the Holy Spirit has been given to us to *convince* us of our sinfulness, *convict* us of the evil we perform, and *convert* us from the addiction to sin. Convincing is not a condemnation so much as a compassionate awakening of our souls to a radical honesty about ourselves. The Spirit imprinted on us the image of God at our conception. In Baptism and Confirmation the Spirit created in us the possibilities of living out all the ideals which being an image of God implies. The Jubilee is a golden opportunity to recover this vision which the Spirit's Love wants to evoke in us.

Yearn for the day that we will journey into eternal life to meet our loving Father, whose desire is to glorify us with divine radiance. The graces of this life already contain the "seeds of glory" which attain their fulfillment in heaven. John Paul says our Jubilee celebration of the Father should include a conversion of our personal lifestyles, a recovery of the richness of God's mercy in the Sacrament of Reconciliation, an opening of our hearts to the mission to all nations, and a readiness to serve the poor. The story of the Prodigal Son is really the tale of a Prodigal Father whose love is matchless and abundant beyond all human imagining. Devotion to our Father is a central key of the Jubilee.

CROSS THE THRESHOLD OF HOPE

Recently, a conversation between Umberto Eco, the author of *The Name of the Rose* and Cardinal Carlo Maria Martini, archbishop of Milan, was published. They were asked to talk about the millennium and address the question "Who's afraid of the Apocalypse?" Eco represented the secular viewpoint while Martini spoke for the world of faith. They found themselves discussing the matter of hope for the future. They laid aside preoccupations with fear and dwelt on matters where all people of good will could work together for the betterment of the world. They agreed that they could collaborate on issues of hope for the future.

Pope John Paul's most accessible book is his own meditation, *Crossing the Threshold of Hope*. Over and over again, he writes, "Be not afraid!" The millennium should not be a scare tactic to frighten people. It ought to be a new opportunity to bring hope to the world, a hope that is best founded in faith in Jesus Christ. The power of Christ's Cross and Resurrection is greater than any evil that one might fear. Grace is mightier than sin.

In all the Easter narratives Jesus repeats, "Don't be scared. Be not afraid." The last words of Jesus heard on earth have to do with banishing fear and giving people hope. Many are scared by what we have produced and created in this world. John Paul says, "Don't be afraid of that." Reach out to Christ whose vision and graces are stronger than any threat we have invented against ourselves. Once this is clear, we shall begin to understand the gift of the third millennium and its enormous potential for good that lies ahead of us.

Be not afraid.

Be filled with hope.

Father Alfred McBride, O. Praem.

PART ONE

THE MILLENNIUM
AS THE END OF TIME

But of that day and hour no one knows,
neither the angels of heaven, nor the Son,
but the Father alone.

— Matthew 24:36

CHAPTER ONE:

SOUND THE ALARM! THE END IS COMING!

He will come again in glory to judge the living and the dead.
— Nicene Creed

In his novel *The Clowns of God*, Morris West imagines that his fictional pope, Gregory XVII has received a vision about the imminent end of the world. The pope had been making a retreat at the Benedictine abbey of Monte Cassino. While sitting in the cloister gardens and meditating on John's Gospel, the pope experienced a trance. He saw a dead planet. A divine flame enveloped him and impregnated him with a message: the end of the world was near.

The pope concluded that God was calling him to announce the Second Coming of Christ. The world must prepare for the last days. When the vision passes, Gregory returns to Rome and confides his revelation to his advisers. They are shocked and dismayed. Popes don't normally have private revelations. If they do, they should keep them to themselves. He can't be serious about telling the world about its end. They consider him to be a walking time bomb. He must be stopped.

Undeterred, Gregory writes an encyclical, "In These Last Fateful Years of the Millennium," which he plans to publish. It opens with these words:

> In these last fateful years of the millennium. . . .
> In this dark time of confusion, violence and

17

terror, I, Gregory, your brother in the flesh, your servant in Jesus Christ, am commanded by the Holy Spirit to write you these words of warning and comfort. . . .

The curial cardinals obtain a copy of the encyclical before he can publish it. It would cause panic and unprecedented world turmoil. He has to be stopped. Unable to convince him to abandon its proclamation, they force his resignation, aided by contrived medical testimony that declares Gregory to be mentally unfit to continue. He is shipped off to virtual house arrest at Monte Cassino.

Eventually, he is permitted to embark on a lonely journey to test the validity of his vision. In case you wish to read the story for yourself to see how it turns out, I will leave it here.

I begin with this story because I think it illustrates our fascination with the millennium. All living creatures eventually die. Will not this world, as we know it, one day cease to be?

The Church broadens our outlook about the end. Every Sunday we pray in the Nicene Creed, "He [Jesus] will come again to judge the living and the dead." Michelangelo painted his Last Judgment on the altar wall of the Sistine Chapel in so vivid a manner that those who see it will never forget it.

In visiting many medieval village churches in England, I was struck by their custom of painting a fresco of the Last Judgment on the back walls of their chapels. This means that the worshipers would always be reminded of this doctrine as they departed their churches after the services. The picture on the wall seeped into their subconscious where the truth mingled with their other understandings of life and death.

Faith connects the end of the world with our eternal destiny. Religion links our moral behavior today with our future with — or without — God.

Because of the year 2000, there is a spontaneous burst of interest in the millennium. Many will use the occasion to feed on our fears. Some like to threaten. It's a shame that so many people enjoy being frightened. Fear mongers usually find an audience because some people enjoy being scared.

On the other hand, just as we normally put our personal deaths out of our minds, so we dislike imagining that this world will cease to be. Psychologists call this "denial." It is considered a protective mechanism. Fear is a tricky emotion. While we need some practical fear such as not putting our hands into a flame, we also must realize that too much dread paralyzes behavior.

In one of his sermons, St. Augustine was railing against the sins of his flock at Hippo. Then he pulled back and felt a surge of sympathy and compassion for his congregation. "I know you see the world as a beautiful place. I understand why you love it so much."

There is a legitimate love for the world because it is a treasure of God's creation. God made the sun to give us light, warmth, and life. God gave us the rain to slake our thirst and cause the trees and the grain to grow. God invented the mountains to lift up our hearts and the oceans to inspire us to wisdom. Naturally we do not want to see it go. Just as we fear to lose our lives, so we dread the loss of creation.

However, some people will exploit our normal fears and spread alarms about the end. Preachers of doom have always been around. I believe our job is to distinguish between those who are manipulating us and those who have a true call from God to awaken our consciences. The prophets of the Bible possessed such a call and often spoke in apocalyptic tones.

Jesus himself delivered apocalyptic sermons just before his death. Yet he clearly said that he did not know when the end of the world would happen. Though he was the Son of God, his Father did not grant him this knowledge in his human consciousness.

> But of that day and hour no one knows, neither the angels of heaven, nor the Son, but the Father alone (Mt 24:36).

As you read this book, I urge you to keep this verse of Scripture clearly in mind. Write it at the beginning of each chapter and look at it each time you read so that you have Christ's perspective on the timing of the end of time. While you might expect preachers, priests, and ministers to deliver talks about the end, you should not be surprised to hear apocalyptic bulletins from secular sources as well. You have all heard about global warming due to holes in the ozone layer and other talk about a nuclear winter. Science is interested in the "end."

ASTRONOMERS DESCRIBE THE END

Astrophysicists Fred Adams and Greg Loughlin claim our world will end, though not soon. They have published their research in an article, "The Dying Universe." For all practical purposes, the universe will end when the stars and our sun stop shining. Humans will be gone before that because the oceans will have boiled away in the sun's dying flameout, reducing the planet to an uninhabitable cinder.

Coincidentally, their prophecy echoes the words of Jesus:

> the sun will be darkened,
>   and the moon will not give its light,
> and the stars will fall from the sky,
>   and the powers of the heavens will be shaken
> (Mt 24:29).

The astronomers tell us there is no need for any immediate concern. The sun will not die until five billion years from now. The process of decay will take an incomprehensible ten trillion trillion trillion years. "That's a Yotta Years," as science writer, Madeline Jacobs puts it.

The following is how they see the future unfolding:

> The sun is expected to die in about five billion years, reduced to an extinct remnant known as a white dwarf. Earth might survive

the solar death throes, but its oceans would boil away from the heat, and life, if it endured that long, would no longer be possible. The sun will not be alone. Slowly, all the larger solar-mass stars will turn to white dwarfs, and the more slowly evolving small red dwarf stars will assume more importance. The end of all star formation should come in 100 trillion years (*New York Times*, January 10, 1997).

Much later comes what they call the Degenerate Era as the stars begin to die off as they burn up their nuclear fuel. Left behind will be stellar remnants. And then, finally, the Dark Era begins. The universe will consist of a sea of electrons, positrons, neutrinos, and radiation. The universe will be totally black.

Genesis says that is how it was just before creation. "The earth was a formless wasteland, and *darkness covered the abyss. . .*" (Gen 1:2; emphasis added).

You may have imagined the universe ending this way, but like most people you probably think it will happen far sooner and much more dramatically, not stretching out over trillions of years. Of course you may still be right.

The scientists are projecting this outcome based on what they know about the laws of physics right now. Such laws are open to revision. The only point I am making here is that we sense this world, as we experience it, will end. Astronomers agree, even if they are not absolutely certain about the time schedule.

I like to remind my readers that the uncertainty of science about the exact timing of the end fits with Christ's own uncertainty. Both agree on the fact of the end. Present science has hunches about the timing, pushing it trillions of years away. But that is an educated guess, not a prediction of absolute certitude.

Still I believe it is important to include the astronomers'

scenarios because they verify that there is a finiteness about the world as we know it. We live within limits. There's something limited about the world as we know it. Faith has more to tell us about this, but more of that later.

THE ATOMIC CLOCK

All during the fifty years of the Cold War (1945-1995) the *Bulletin of Atomic Scientists* placed an atomic clock on the cover of their magazine. When the perils of this "war" increased, the minute hand moved closer to midnight; as the threat lessened, the hand moved backwards. During those fearful years the minute hand wavered between ten to two minutes to midnight. It was an apocalyptic reminder. It was our own modern, secular icon of the Last Judgment.

If the truth be known, you don't have to wait for Mother Nature to take her good old time to unwind the universe. We are perfectly capable of hastening the process and vaporizing the world right now. We have the tools of nuclear destruction.

On August 6, 1945, we dropped an atomic bomb on Hiroshima. Need I remind you this was the feast of the Transfiguration of the Lord? The white heat of the bomb destroyed and killed. The blinding light of Christ was creative and saving and life-giving.

The explosion of the bomb created an area of destruction extending two miles in all directions. Nearly 200,000 people died. Twenty-six out of thirty-three fire stations were destroyed. Only three of the city's forty-five hospitals survived. The heaviest casualties were among children.

The young Father Pedro Arrupe, who would one day become the Father General of the Jesuits, was near the city that day. He remembers that the blast stopped his wall clock. He later wrote in his book *A Planet to Heal*:

> For me, that silent and motionless clock has become a symbol. The explosion of the first atomic bomb has become a para-historical

phenomenon. It is not a memory. It is a perpetual experience outside of history which does not pass with the ticking of a clock. The pendulum stopped and Hiroshima has remained engraved on my mind. It belongs to motionless eternity.

During the Cold War, the United States and Russia built a vast arsenal of atomic weapons. Our foreign policy was called MAD (Mutually Assured Destruction). This attitude of deterrence claimed that we would have "peace through strength." Today there are meetings about nuclear disarmament — and there has been some success. The American bishops issued a Pastoral Letter on War and Peace in which they asked our leaders to reconsider our nuclear policy.

The nuclear age is an age of moral as well as physical danger. We are the first generation since Genesis with the power to virtually destroy God's creation. We cannot remain silent in the face of such danger. Why do we address these issues? We are simply trying to live up to the call of Jesus to be peacemakers in our own time and situation.

What are we saying? Fundamentally, we are saying that decisions about nuclear weapons are among the most pressing moral questions of our age. We are saying that good ends — defending one's country, protecting freedom, etc. — cannot justify immoral means and the use of weapons that kill indiscriminately and threaten whole societies.

Pope John Paul II added his own comment later, "The logic of nuclear deterrence cannot be considered a final goal or an appropriate and secure means for safeguarding international peace." The bishops and the pope have attempted to lift the discussion beyond politics and diplomacy to a moral and spiritual level. The issue is fundamentally a moral one. We must be capable of acting out of firm moral principles.

There is such a thing as a moral code and an objective moral vision. History's lessons are clear. When a civilization and a culture abandon morality, then self-destruction follows. Gibbon's *Decline and Fall of the Roman Empire* is a classic study of how inner corruption caused the demise of a magnificent civilization. The enemy within is far stronger than the enemy without.

I think it is no mistake that once again the great moral parable of the Titanic captures our imagination. Both in a Broadway musical and a Hollywood film, we once again live out a testimony to human arrogance and pride that issued in a terrible tragedy. The so-called unsinkable ship clashed with an iceberg. Like the proud Tower of Babel, that poor ship crumbled and died.

Morality matters. It is because of that we will hear a lot of apocalyptic language today, for we are indeed in a moral crisis that needs to be addressed. I am not prepared nor qualified to say the world will end tomorrow, but I agree that we should take our moral temperature so that our own cherished culture will not repeat the self-destructive performance of other times.

We all need to remember that nuclear weapons are not only entrenched at this moment in concrete silos in Montana and Siberia but are also lodged in the minds of international leaders. Our President is still near the red box and the button that could summon the firing of our missiles. Tempers are cooler today, thank God, but in the background lingers the danger.

Let us hope we have the breathing time to put our religious, moral, and spiritual houses in order. No other fact dramatizes the question before us. Have we come at last from the creation story in Genesis to the vision of the end described in the last chapters of the Apocalypse?

THE CLASH OF CIVILIZATIONS

As the year 2000 approaches, Christians and secularists alike are theorizing about scary futures. I will discuss various Christian opinions about the end of history in another chapter and will offer what I believe to be the correct approach as found in sober Catholic teaching toward the end of this book.

Let me share with you here a secular apocalypse outlined in Samuel Huntington's *The Clash of Civilizations and the Remaking of the World Order*. Huntington is a Harvard political scientist. He argues that the next great war will not be based on ideologies such as communism and democracy but on the resurgence of tribal and religious-based civilizations.

The fault line among these civilizations will be the sources of war. One culture to watch as the year 2000 rolls around is Islam. One out of every five people on earth prays to Allah. Islam is no longer content to be the forgotten "belly of the world" stretching from Indonesia to Morocco. Increasingly, it wants a bigger piece of the global pie.

Looming just as large as Islam is an emerging and militant China. Huntington forecasts that World War III will begin with China invading Vietnam to take its oil. The United States will attempt to intervene but will be frustrated when Japan declares it will remain neutral. Chaos will result.

India will attack Muslim Pakistan but will find itself attacked by Muslim Iran. The Arabs will invade Israel. China will force Japan to join the war against the United States. All major civilizations will mobilize for war. Matters in the United States will be complicated by the phenomenal growth of Hispanics within its borders. The Hispanics are so alienated that a civil war and the threat of national dissolution become possible. If nuclear destruction or biological warfare enters the picture, it is a truly frightening scenario.

Huntington sees this process beginning with the year 2000 and extending well into the twenty-first century. He does not seem to be saying that all this will definitely happen, so much as speculating that it could occur if world leaders fail to understand the expansionist aggression based on culture and civilization such as found in Islamic countries and China. It should be recognized and defused before it gets out of hand.

People who take the Book of Revelation literally would have little trouble seeing in Huntington's vision the arrival of the predicted tribulations so vividly described by St. John. But whether these are the signs of the end of history remains to be seen.

THE NOAH PRECEDENT

I wish to conclude this first chapter with a reflection on the Noah story, which describes an apocalyptic event at the beginning of our history.

In his early career, Bill Cosby popularized the Noah story in his customary humorous manner. He presented Noah first as a doubter and then as a hard-pressed suburban husband building an ark in his neighbor's driveway. With a true comic touch, Cosby pictured the human predicament in which Noah found himself: doubt in the face of the demands of faith, and harassment in trying to do what faith required of him.

Noah ignored the mocking of his neighbors who thought the flood would never come. He completed the ark because he believed God would be true to his word. He probably felt a bit silly building a boat on dry land with no water nearby. This faith test of Noah is a prelude to that which Abraham later experienced (see Hebrews 11:17).

Once the ark was built, Noah and his family and the animals entered the ark. God shut the door after them. God sealed and protected his friends against the coming storm. Biblical accounts of the severity of the flood vary. One speaks of a forty-day rainstorm. "For forty days and forty nights heavy rain poured down upon the earth" (Gen 7:12). Another narrative describes a disastrous worldwide flood. "Higher and higher above the earth rose the waters, until all the highest mountains everywhere were submerged" (Gen 7:19).

It looked as though the world would return to the chaos from which it had been created. But God remembered Noah. God curbed the rush to chaos before Noah and his group were destroyed. And the ark found a resting place. The Hebrew word for rest is *nuah*, which as you can see is a pun based on the name Noah. In the faithful and heroic Noah, rest and peace return to the earth.

It was a common custom among ancient seamen to send forth birds to test for land sites. Noah had no success with the first bird. It had to return. The second, a dove, was more successful. It brought back an olive branch in its beak. The olive branch of peace signaled the departure of angry judgment and the hope of deliverance. The third bird, also a dove, was sent forth and did not come back. Then Noah knew he could live on the earth again.

The first thing Noah did after leaving the ark was to offer a sacrifice. Hence, the first human act on the liberated earth was an act of adoration. The liturgical act celebrated the cleansing of the earth. So awesome was this moment that Noah remained absolutely silent. God "smelled" the sacrifice and was pleased with the sweetness of the gift and with those who offered it. "When the Lord smelled the sweet odor, he said to himself, 'Never again will I doom the earth because of man. . .

> As long as the earth lasts
>   seedtime and harvest,
>   cold and heat,
> Summer and winter,
>   and day and night
>   shall not cease' "
> (Gen 8: 21-22).

Chapter nine of Genesis pictures the covenant between God and Noah. The scene looks like a new creation. God summons man to be fruitful and multiply. People would control the animal world and could kill animals for food.

God concluded a covenant between himself and Noah. God put a sign of the covenant in the heavens. It was wrought out of the colors of the rainbow, a warm and promising assurance that God's grace would never be missing from the earth. It was a rainbow covenant that drew all people to scan the skies for the peace that comes after a storm, to a divine constancy that would never fail, to a gracious God who can never forget his word.

The Hebrew word from which we take the word rainbow usually means "bow of war." Hence what primitive Hebrews understood was that God had pledged to set aside his "bow and arrow" of war and not threaten creation again with chaos. The appearance of the rainbow signaled the restoration of the order of nature.

As God began to heal the universe, shutting off the ocean "above the skies" and limiting the approach of the sea below, he would continue his work of reconciliation in the stormy seas of the human condition on earth. It is a work of salvation that would find its greatest expression in God's Son, Jesus Christ.

The Noah story gives us the context for approaching today's millennial fears. The flood and chaos resulted from the self-destructive immorality of the people of Noah's time. "When the Lord saw how great was man's wickedness on earth . . . he regretted that he had made man on earth, and his heart was grieved" (Gen 6:5-6).

Scripture interprets the catastrophes that nearly ended the world as the inevitable outcome of the self-destructiveness of sin and evil. Yet God did not want his creation destroyed because of human evil. Even amid the coming doom, God rescued a faithful family and the seed animals needed for a future humanity. God watched over this ark of salvation and brought it safely home. Finally the Lord asked the world to consider the rainbow as a sign of his peaceful and loving and protective regard for creation.

This was the first of the major covenant events between God and humanity. It presents God as determined to save us, almost in spite of ourselves. One important fact to notice is that the first apocalypse in recorded Scripture did not result in the obliteration of either the world or humanity. In spite of popular belief, the final apocalyptic scenes in the Book of Revelation do not present any annihilation of the universe or humanity either. There are many dramatic tribulations, of course, and their purpose we shall see in due time.

A lesson I often draw from the Noah Precedent is that God thinks a lot more of us than we do of ourselves. I hear a lot of talk about self-esteem and self-worth and the need for proper self-love. With this I have no great quarrel, except that the means to achieve this often are insufficient. But one thing I do know is that no one will ever love himself or herself as much as God loves us. Each of us needs a decent self-regard, yet none of us will ever appreciate ourselves with the affectionate tenderness God has for us. It is faith in this divine love for us that could tide us through real or imagined apocalypses.

Nelson Mandela shared this truth with us in a unique statement during his inauguration as President of South Africa:

> Our deepest fear is not that we are inadequate. Our deepest fear is that we are powerful beyond measure. It is our light, not our darkness, that most frightens us. We ask ourselves who are we to be brilliant, gorgeous, talented, fabulous? Actually, who are we not to be? We are a child of God. Our playing small doesn't serve the world. We were born to manifest the glory of God that is within us; it is in Everyone! And as we let our own light shine, we unconsciously give other people permission to do the same. As we are liberated from our own fear, our presence automatically liberates others!

Chapter Two:

Is the Antichrist Knocking at Your Door?

Children, it is the last hour; and just as you heard that the antichrist was coming, so now many antichrists have appeared.
— 1 John 2:18

Hal Lindsey must be one of the world's most satisfied authors. His book *The Late Great Planet Earth* has sold more than twenty-five million copies. Lindsey is associated with Dallas Theological Seminary, a center for millennial thinking. The success of his book proves that millions of people believe that we can pinpoint the time when the antichrist will appear — and therefore the time when the Christ will come. The year 2000 is too tempting to overlook. A temporal millennium seems like the right time to expect the divine millennium.

Like his fellow millennialists, Lindsey believes that biblical prophecy took a holiday for almost two thousand years. Between the destruction of Jerusalem, including fall of the Second Temple in A.D. 70 and the restoration of the Jewish State in 1948, biblical prophecy lay dormant. In other words, these prophecies work only when Israel is a political entity.

These believers separate the history of Israel from the history of the "true church," apparently meaning their own faith persuasions. They have created a "postponement theory" in which the prophecies, left unfulfilled when the Jews rejected Jesus and lost Jerusalem and the Temple, had to wait for completion until the return of the Jews to Palestine. The prophetic clock stopped in A.D. 70 and did not start ticking again until 1948.

Lindsey claims that the last fifty years provide us with numerous signs of the approaching tribulations and the antichrist. The explosion of the atomic bomb, Russia's interest in the Middle East, the rise of the European Common Market — above all, the emergence of the state of Israel — are the major signs of the coming apocalypse. Lindsey denies knowing the exact date of this event, but at the same time estimated the process would begin in 1988.

The activity of the European Common Market, according to Lindsey, would result in a ten-nation "United States" of Europe. This union would be the modern equivalent of ancient Rome. It would provide the power base for the coming dictator, the antichrist. He would sign a treaty with Israel which would enable the Jews to rebuild the Temple.

The antichrist will be revealed when he is miraculously healed of a head wound. He will then enthrone himself in the Temple as God. This event will repeat the erection of the statue of Zeus in the second Temple, by Antiochus IV, an experience described in the Book of Daniel. Devout Jews in biblical times recoiled from this desecration of their temple and called it the "abomination of desolation."

Lindsey's account goes on to say that the antichrist will have a colleague, a Jewish false prophet, who will compel all people to worship the dictator. Lindsey creates this scenario out of Apocalypse 13:11-18, where the world ruler is called "the beast." His accomplice will execute anyone who does not adore the beast. He will "force all the people, small and great, rich and poor, free and slave, to be given a stamped image on their right hands, or their foreheads" (Rev 13:16).

Lindsey has produced a book that mixes biblical prophecy and political commentary. Playing upon millennial fears, he offers his readers a way to make sense out of contemporary political developments with literal applications of various biblical prophecies to the changing world scene. If there is concern about the "new world order," he gives it a name and an ominous destiny. The battles of the Cold War are over, but beware, Armageddon looms in the near future.

In an update of his earlier work, Lindsey predicts that China will invade Israel with 200 million soldiers. The mother of all battles will follow. The whole world will be engulfed in a nuclear holocaust that will threaten the planet itself. At this point Christ will return, leading an army of angels. The final judgment will follow with salvation only for those who accept Jesus as their personal savior. At the close of this chapter I will offer some reflections on this scenario.

I believe that we need now to examine the biblical theme of the antichrist. What does Scripture say?

BIBLICAL TEACHING ABOUT THE ANTICHRIST

The actual term "antichrist" appears only in the first and second letters of John:

> Children, it is the last hour; and just as you heard the antichrist was coming, so now many antichrists have appeared (1 Jn 2:18).

> Whoever denies the Father and the Son, this is the antichrist (1 Jn 2:22).

> and every spirit that does not acknowledge Jesus does not belong to God. This is the spirit of the antichrist. . . (1 Jn 4:3).

> Many deceivers have gone out into the world, those who do not acknowledge Jesus Christ as coming in the flesh; such is the deceitful one and the antichrist (2 Jn 7).

The idea of an antichrist also appears in other texts. The second letter to the Thessalonians (2:3-12), describes the antichrist as the "lawless one," who will persecute believers just prior to Christ's Second Coming. Apocalypse chapters twelve and thirteen call the antichrist, the "beast" and spell out the terrors and threats he will enact against Christians.

Apocalyptic passages in the Old Testament provide the origins for belief in an antichrist. Prophets envisioned a final struggle between those faithful to God (Israel) and those hostile to him (pagan nations). This war will culminate in an epic struggle at the end of history. God will win the battle that will be accompanied by cosmic signs and disturbances.

What is the story behind the story of Old Testament apocalyptic thinking?

You may recall that the Jewish people were conquered and taken into exile by the Babylonians. This "captivity" was ended by Cyrus, king of the Persians, who allowed them to go home about 539 B.C. They were given religious freedom and a kind of "home rule" based on laws developed by Ezra the scribe. But they were not given real political freedom or the permission to have their own king. So began their longing for the return of the House of David and an anointed king — a messiah — who would win their independence.

In 330 B.C., Alexander the Great conquered Israel and all the adjacent lands. After he died, his kingdom was divided among his generals. Egypt ruled Israel for the next hundred years. Then Syrian Greeks wrested Israel from the Egyptians. The Syrian king, Antiochus IV, treated the Jewish people cruelly, and he insisted they adopt Greek cultural customs which meant abandoning circumcision and traditional dietary laws. He was the one who installed a statue of Zeus in the Temple and sacrificed pigs (an unclean animal in the eyes of Jews) to the god. It was a sacrilege.

His offensive behavior and his persecution generated a rebellion led by a country priest in 167 B.C. Judas Maccabeus and his brothers drove the Syrian Greeks out of Jerusalem and re-consecrated the Temple. The Maccabees became the new rulers and assumed the titles of high priest and even king. The problem was that they did not descend from a family of authorized priests nor of the royal line of kings. Worse yet, their successors became corrupt.

The Pharisees opposed them for all these reasons. They lost popular support because of their immoral lives. It was in these one hundred fifty years before Christ that an intense longing for an anointed king of the line of David grew in the people who wanted real political independence as well as religious purity.

The literature that became the focus for these nationalist and religious hopes is called apocalyptic or revelational writing. Oppressed and disappointed Jews needed a literature of hope. They were rewarded with the Book of Daniel and parts of the Book of Ezekiel. These works are full of brilliant and often scary imagery and the promise of the ultimate victory of good over evil. Many extra-biblical apocalypses also appeared in these years.

Apocalyptic writing stressed the appearance of a false messiah or antichrist. Some of this resulted from the influence of the Persians, who believed in a dualistic religion in which there were two gods, one good and the other evil, always in conflict. The figure of Satan, a fallen angel, sometimes assumed the mantle of a god seemingly as powerful as the good God. Satan donned the cloak of the super-rebel and leader of the vast army of the devils.

Scripture is always careful to protect the supreme authority of God, but in popular religion Satan seemed to be almost as powerful as God, if not actually as strong. More to the point for our purposes, Satan seemed to be embodied in human rulers such as Antiochus IV. He is not yet called antichrist, but he is clearly anti-God.

The story is first played out in Ezekiel, chapters 38-39. The nations of the earth assemble under the leadership of Gog from the land of Magog. Gog has all the traits of Israel's many persecutors. His armies come from the north, the source of so many invasions in previous history. His army is composed of troops from the four corners of the world. But God strikes the bows and arrows from their hands. The invaders are slaughtered on the mountains of Israel. The birds and beasts feed on their flesh.

Gog is an individual, but not a historical figure. He embodies the leadership of forces hostile to God's people. The story is a parable of God's final vindication of his people. Their longing for religious purity and royal independence will be satisfied by God's victory over evil. Gog is the first hint of an antichrist in biblical literature. He will appear again in Revelation 20:8, where he is simply the symbol of the four corners of the earth bent on destroying the new people of God.

The apocalyptic story is told again in bolder and more specific language in the Book of Daniel. In chapter seven of Daniel, the prophet has a vision of four beasts: a lion, a bear, a leopard, and one so terrifying, horrible, and strong that an animal like it had not been seen before. These four beasts represent the four empires that had oppressed Israel: Babylonians, Medes, Persians, and Greeks.

The fourth one was the worst and represented the Greek dominance. It had ten horns, referring to the ten rulers before Antiochus IV, represented by the "little horn." Horns are symbols of power and force. Considering how much Antiochus was hated, it is odd that he would he symbolized by a small horn.

I would ask you to put a "bookmark" by the ten horns, because modern millennialists see in this image from Daniel a prophecy of the ten great powers of a United Europe which would result from the European Common Market over whom a dictator-antichrist will rule. In fact they see the "little horn" as the antichrist himself.

Daniel sees a heavenly courtroom. God appears as the Ancient One on a throne. Snow bright robes adorn him and white hair crowns his head. Wheels of burning fire whir around him and thousands of angels stand ready to do his bidding. God calls the court to order and the court's books are opened and the charges read against the beasts. They are sentenced to destruction.

In verse fourteen we see the Son of Man coming on the clouds right up to the throne of the Ancient One. "He received dominion, glory and kingship." All peoples of every language shall serve him. His dominion will never be taken away. In other words, God will give Israel a Messiah to replace the beasts. They will have their kingdom.

Evil will lose.

It was only natural that the Israelite readers were assured this meant the restoration of the royal line of David. The Son of Man would be a Davidic king who would remove all foreign oppression. We know from the Gospels that Jesus identified himself often with this Son of Man and just as clearly taught that his kingdom was not of this world. This is most evident in his meeting with Pilate during the Passion.

Daniel's pictures of the beasts will show up again in Revelation. Now the great beast is the Roman Empire and specifically refers to Nero. The author has composed another book of hope, this time for a persecuted Christian community that fears the young Church will be destroyed by the Roman Empire. Just as God had delivered Israel from Antiochus IV, so now Christ will save the Christian Church from the likes of Nero and Domitian (the emperor in charge at the time of that writing). Here are the new antichrists who will strut their hour upon the stage of history and then be seen no more.

This brief overview of why apocalyptic thinking appeared in Scripture should help you see its relevance to biblical people. Before examining its pertinence to us today, I would like to place before you some images of the antichrist which appeared throughout history.

WHAT WILL THE ANTICHRIST LOOK LIKE?

Believe it or not, the Irish developed one of the most popular pictures of the antichrist in the tenth century on the eve of the first millennium. It begins with the legend of the phoenix and argues that the risen phoenix is actually the woman who gave birth to the antichrist.

The phoenix is a bird which builds its nest for seventy-two years. No one can understand such mysteries and the adornment he makes from his feathers, as well a the sound from his singing. A fire comes from heaven and burns the nest and tree and makes ashes on the earth. Rain comes from Africa and puts out the fire. From the ash and rain will be born the girl from whom the antichrist will come. Two young virgin girls will stand there, called Abilia and Lapidia, from whose breasts will pour the milk by which they will nourish him for five years. When the five years are completed, he will begin to reign (Bernard McGinn, *Antichrist*, Harper, San Francisco, p.98)

This birth story of the antichrist, based on the phoenix myth, now adopts a scriptural quality. The next scene is an imaginary one in which the disciples are having a discussion with Jesus about the physical appearance of the antichrist.

His disciples said to Jesus: 'Lord, tell us what he will be like.' And Jesus said to them: 'His stature will be nine cubits. He will have black hair pulled up like an iron chain. In his forehead he will have one eye shining like the dawn. His lower lip will be large, he will have no upper lip. On his hand the little finger will be the longer. His left foot will be wider. He will come to the sea and say, "Dry up," and it will be dried. He says to the sun, "Stand," and it will stop. And he says to the moon, "Become dark," and it will be darkened. And the stars will fall from heaven' (McGinn, *Antichrist*, p. 98).

History's picture of the antichrist begins simply with a man taking the role as in the case of Gog. This view is repeated in the second chapter of 2 Thessalonians. The people are convinced that Christ's Second Coming is about to happen. St. Paul urges them to calm down. He tells them that the end of the world will only happen after a "great apostasy" and the revelation of the "lawless one" who will sit in God's temple and claim he is god (see 2:3-4).

Paul's listeners will be remembering how Antiochus IV conquered Israel and set up a statue of Zeus in their Temple. In disgust their ancestors had called it an abomination (see Daniel 12:11). This anti-god becomes an antichrist in the person of a lawless one.

But very quickly the image assumes monster-like qualities in the Book of Revelation, chapters twelve through thirteen. A woman giving birth appears, clothed with the sun, crowned with stars and the moon under her feet. A fiery dragon appears and attempts to devour her newborn child. Then the dragon becomes a leviathan, a sea monster. No sooner has this figure appeared than it is changed into a behemoth, a landmonster. These fearful monstrous pictures are meant to show how horrible, powerful, and threatening the antichrist will be.

Subsequent history will linger on these fantastic ways of portraying the antichrist. The Irish image of a hideous man, mentioned above, is a typical variation of a theme initiated in Apocalypse. But in our own times, the antichrist is once again a mere man, acting monstrously, but cleverly.

Now he will be good looking, charming, seductive (like the snake in Genesis?). He will have remarkable political know-how. He will insinuate himself into Euro-politics until he becomes master of the game, a hugely attractive leader who takes over the control of Europe. He won't breathe fire, or have scaly skin, or slimy breath. He will have a London tailor, French manners, Italian smoothness, and a German personal trainer. He will be a man perfectly suited to satellite television and the internet. He will be just as brutish as Nero, Hitler, and Stalin, just as intent on destroying Christ as they were, but his method will be disarming. He will be the ultimate Trojan Horse, a "gift" let into the heart of civilization, and just as deadly. Read Michael O'Brien's *Father Elijah*, or Malachi Martin's *Windswept House*, for novelistic versions of this contemporary antichrist.

WELL, WHAT ARE WE TO THINK?

Scripture is quite insistent that a false messiah or antichrist will usher in the last days of history. Scripture also teaches that there will be other antichrists in times of historical crisis for God's people. We need to make a distinction between the end of "a" world and the final end of "the" world as we know it.

The antichrist will come at the end of "the" world we know. Other antichrists will arrive at the end of "a" particular world.

For example, the early Christian community suffered for three centuries at the hands of Roman emperors. But freedom came in 313. Jesus triumphed over evil and delivered our people from persecution. That was the end of "a" world.

This pattern appears again and again. In the fourteenth century, when the Black Plague killed more than a third of Europe's population, it was easy for people to conclude that history was coming to an end. But it didn't. Wandering preachers, acting as "messiahs," scolded the people and predicted that the final cataclysm was imminent. It didn't happen. The plague subsided and a historical era passed.

During the thirty-year religious wars that followed the Reformation, with the suffering and persecution that accompanied it, people wondered again if the world was closing down. It was during this period that some people began calling the pope the antichrist. Once more, however, peace broke out and another era ended.

In our own day both Nazism and communism, with their ferocious persecution of religion, reawakened the title of antichrist, which was easily applied to Hitler and Stalin. Perhaps never in history have the signs of the Apocalypse been so evident, yet that era also has passed into the chronicles of history. Jesus was victorious over the enemies of faith, and the community of believers is stronger for it.

Jesus foresaw that antichrists would come not only at the end of history, but throughout the history of the Church. They will be more subtle than the tyrants we can easily identify. In this sense, the current millennialists have a point in picturing the antichrist as an elegant political leader.

"Many false prophets will arise and deceive many. . . . If anyone says to you then, 'Look here is the Messiah!' or, 'There he is!' do not believe it. False messiahs and false prophets will arise, and they will perform signs and wonders so great as to deceive, if it were possible, even the elect" (Mt 24:11, 23-24).

So then, what are we to think? We certainly can agree with the millennialists that an antichrist will arise at the end of history. He may either be a tyrant-beast or a more clever leader posing as a messiah. We do not know. Where I would disagree with the present and fervent millennialists is their self-assured scenario that the end is about to happen. How do they know? I believe they do not take seriously enough the words of Jesus, "For you do not know on which day your Lord will come" (Mt 24:42).

I also find their wedding of biblical prophecy to political analysis too arbitrary. They keep changing the players. Until recently, Russia was the key player. Now it is China. They must keep torturing the text to make the ten horns of Daniel precisely fit an ever-changing political situation in Europe.

Further, I do not think it is respectful of Jewish history to bypass nearly two thousand years of their history, from A.D. 70 to 1948, in order to have a neat connection between biblical prophecy and the emergence of the state of Israel. Jews did not cease to be a covenant people in A.D.70. Through the centuries they worshipped and prayed and struggled and did what they could to live the Torah and the Mitzvah (the commandments). I do not believe it serves any useful purpose to put them at the flashpoint of Armageddon either at the year 2000 or some comparable date in the foreseeable future. They may rightly agree with the old rabbi who said, "Lord, protect me from my friends. I can handle my enemies much more easily."

My final misgiving with the present millennial fervor is a discomfort with the fear and threat it generates on the one hand, and the self-confident smugness of the "saved" it fosters on the other hand. I know history will end. I believe Jesus will come to usher in the new creation. I just don't know when it will happen. I believe my job is to be a believing, witnessing, and practicing Catholic every hour of every day. I fully accept Christ's advice, "Stay awake!" (Mt 24:42).

That is better than futile speculation.

CHAPTER THREE:

GET READY FOR THE RAPTURE

A Cardinal: "Holy Father, the end of the world is coming.
        What shall we do?"
The Pope: "Look busy."

The teaching on rapture by millennialists comes from an expansive reading of St. Paul's first letter to the Thessalonians.

> For the Lord himself, with a word of command, with the voice of an archangel and with the trumpet of God, will come down from heaven, and the dead in Christ will rise first. Then we who are alive, who are left, will be caught up together with them in the clouds to meet the Lord in the air. Thus we shall always be with the Lord (1 Thes 4:16-17).

Writers with vivid imaginations have little trouble picturing this scene. Marble tombs will explode as the dead bodies of resurrected saints rise to meet Jesus coming in glory. Cars will stand empty on the interstates, engines still running, as their drivers disappear. Food will boil on stoves but no one will be there to eat this earthly dinner. Believers will have departed to dine at the marriage supper of the lamb.

Dr. John Hagee, pastor of the Cornerstone Church in San Antonio, Texas, has his own colorful description of the world's reaction to the rapture.

> Newspapers will scream, MILLIONS MISS-ING WITH NO EXPLANATION. TV stations

43

will broadcast live from local neighborhoods and cemeteries, and their cameras will capture empty graves, ruptured mausoleums, silent homes, wrecked cars. They'll interview neighbors who dab their eyes with tissue and exclaim, "I was right here talking to Mr. Jones and suddenly he disappeared. Right in front of my eyes, I tell you. He was here and then he vaporized! Like something out of *Star Trek*, but faster!"

Nightline will feature a panel of esteemed educators, philosophers, and clergymen who will attempt to explain what happened. The token psychologist will declare that the world is experiencing unprecedented mass hysteria. The venerable theologian will jabber about "right-wing, Bible thumping, politically-incorrect hate mongers" who believed an invalid and nonsensical theory called the Rapture.

Telephone lines around the world will jam as families try to check on their loved ones. And the churches of the world will be packed with weeping, hysterical people who see the truth too late and cry, "The Lord of glory has come and we are left behind to go through the Tribulation and to face the coming Antichrist" (John Hagee, *Beginning of the End*, Thomas Nelson Publishers, Nashville, 1996, pp. 104-105).

How did these two verses from Paul's first letter to the Thessalonians become such a flamboyant source for millennialists? The term "rapture" does not appear in Scripture. The word appears as an explanatory note in the *Scofield Reference Bible* edited in 1909 by a minister, Cyrus Scofield.

He interpreted the words "caught up" as the "rapture of the Church." As a verb the word means "to seize or snatch" (from the Latin *rapere*). As a noun, it implies ecstasy or rapture.

The popularity of the idea of the rapture may be traced back to a minister, John Nelson Darby, in the 1830s. This was a time when many American Christians founded renewal movements intended to transform America into an earthly "kingdom of God." Darby connected the rapture to the millennium, or thousand-year reign of Christ on earth (see Revelation 20). Christ's Second Coming will occur prior to this thousand-year reign. Faithful believers will join Christ in this rule which precedes final salvation in heaven.

How is the rapture story being proclaimed today?

Robert Baldwin describes their story succinctly in his thoughtful book *The End of the World: A Catholic View* (Our Sunday Visitor, Inc., 1984). I summarize his excellent narrative here.

Modern millenarians predict that the rapture will come just before a seven-year tribulation. Their churches call themselves pre-millennial or pre-tribs. Very soon (though the date keeps changing) Jesus will come to rapture his church. All true believers will be caught up in the air and taken to heaven with him. Meanwhile seven years of tribulation will afflict the earth. The sun will be darkened, stars will fall, lakes will turn to blood. People on earth will suffer as never in history.

During this period the antichrist will come. He will be an attractive man and appeal to most people. With the help of a false prophet he will become ruler of the world and set up his headquarters in the newly built temple in Jerusalem. His number will be 666. This mark of the "beast" will be worn or tatooed on one's forehead in order to be able to buy or sell things. All resisters will be executed. Many will realize what happened to the Christians who disappeared in the rapture and will yearn to be in heaven with them. Numerous Jews will embrace Christianity and await the Second Coming.

But before the parousia (Second Coming) there will be the

final war of history, the battle of Armageddon. Two hundred million soldiers, led by the kings of the east (Red China?) will launch an assault on Jerusalem. At the decisive moment of that battle, Jesus will come with the raptured believers and defeat the invaders. The angels will throw the antichrist and his false prophet into a lake of fire. Angels will bind Satan in a bottomless pit.

Now for a thousand years, Jesus and the raptured Christians will rule the world and give it a thousand years of peace, not known since the time of Adam and Eve in paradise before the Fall. At the end of the millennium, Satan will be released and permitted to tempt the believers who accepted Christ after the rapture. Those who give in to Satan will be sent to hell forever. The earth will be consumed by fire and replaced with a new heaven and a new earth where the redeemed will live with Christ forever.

This is the basic story line about the rapture, the tribulations, the millennium, and the end of the world as we know it. I should note that among millennialists there is a major dispute caused by the post-millennial believers. In their view the sequence of the last things goes this way: The world will move toward a thousand years of peace. After this will come the tribulations and then the rapture and the end of the world. This view was popular in the nineteenth century, while the pre-millennials have the prevailing edge today.

In evaluating this complicated view of the rapture, we should take a close look at the first epistle to the Thessalonians to see what Paul was really saying.

WHAT DID PAUL REALLY SAY TO THE THESSALONIANS?

When St. Paul began his mission to Europe he established his first church in Philippi, a lovely city in northern Greece. When he had sufficient confidence in their ability to carry on without him he traveled east about ninety miles to Thessalonica (or Thessaloniki as it is called today). He preached in the local synagogue and made enough converts from the Jews, gentiles, and women to form a community. Scripture says he was there for "three sabbaths" or three weeks. But the Bible also says he started a tent-making business for his own support, implying his stay there was probably longer (see 1 Thessalonians 2:9-10).

Once they had some stability, he traveled several hundred miles south to Athens and then to Corinth, where he set up a thriving church. Wondering how well his northern community was doing, he sent Timothy up to Thessalonica to strengthen the new Christians in the faith and attach them more closely to the apostles.

Timothy discovered three pastoral problems that needed Paul's fatherly guidance.

First, the Thessalonians believed that Christ's Second Coming would happen very soon. They were not unusual in this. Only twenty years before, Jesus had ascended into heaven. People were still alive who had seen Jesus, and the Christians of that first phase of Christianity wanted to see Christ again. Jesus had promised to return in glory. It was widely held that his Second Coming would occur very soon. Some of the Thessalonians had already quit their jobs. Why bother working when they were about to be transported into heaven?

Second, the Thessalonians wondered what would happen to their relatives and friends who had already died. How would they be saved? They were grieving and confused and did not understand what would happen to the deceased. They had received the fundamentals of the faith, but they needed help in applying their faith to new pastoral problems.

Third, they put too much emphasis on the doctrine of the Second Coming to the point where they were ignoring the rest of Gospel teaching. They did not yet appreciate the fact that a believer gains balance by embracing the whole Gospel and its interpretation by the Church.

Paul wrote two letters to them and addressed each of the issues they raised.

(1) He agreed with them that there will be a Second Com-

ing of Jesus. Paul used the common apocalyptic imagery of the day to illustrate this. Angels will appear and sound the last trumpet. Jesus will arrive on clouds in glory. The believers will be swept up to heaven with him. The believers who have died will rise from their graves. Their bodies will be united to their souls and they will be with Christ forever in heaven.

Paul's use of sky pictures was based on the worldview of the day, which imagined that the blue sky was actually a solid dome, above which was heaven where the Trinity, the Blessed Mother, the angels, and the saints dwelt. He combined the resurrection of the bodies of the just who had died with the ascension of the believers who were alive on earth. He used visuals which fitted the mentality of the times. Today we know that our sky is not solid but rather a space that goes for billions of miles in all direction. Heaven is not a physical space in our sense of the word.

Later Paul will modify his description of the general resurrection and simply speak of it as a mystery and use a seed-plant comparison for the resurrection of the dead. "Behold I tell you a mystery" (1 Cor 15:51). We know we will rise from the dead and that those still living will be transformed as well. We do not know exactly how this will happen. Take time to read 1 Corinthians 15:35-58 where Paul gives a stirring teaching on the resurrection of the dead and the spiritual transformation of all believers.

(2) As to those Thessalonians who had walked away from their jobs because the Second Coming would happen any day, Paul rebukes them for their irresponsibility. They should continue with their Christian duties and a life that witnesses the teachings of Jesus to everyone. "We hear that some are conducting themselves among you in a disorderly way, by not keeping busy but minding the business of others" (2 Thes 3:11). ". . . If anyone [is] unwilling to work, neither should that one eat" (2 Thes 3:10). The doctrine of the Second Coming is not an excuse for irresponsibility.

(3) As for those Thessalonians who were overanxious about

the immediate coming of Jesus, Paul modifies his first letter to them by adding stages to the parousia. It will be preceded by an apostasy and then the arrival of the "lawless one."

> We ask you, brothers, with regard to the coming of our Lord Jesus Christ and our assembling with him, not to be shaken out of your minds . . . or by a letter allegedly from us that the day of the Lord is at hand. . . . For unless the apostasy comes first and the lawless one is revealed, the one doomed to perdition, who opposes and exalts himself above every so-called god. . . [the parousia will not be at hand] (bracketed words added) (2 Thes 2:1-4).

In this passage Paul is slowing down the expectation of the Second Coming. He wants to temper their fervor and urge them to focus on daily life and its demands and to witness Christ to one another and the world. The full Gospel needs attention, not just one doctrine. In his first letter he affirmed and identified with their expectations of the parousia. In his second letter he introduced a longer-range scenario, borrowing from Old Testament apocalyptic writing about an anti-god such as Gog or Antiochus IV, which I described for you in chapter two.

It should be remembered that the early Church was in a formative stage. The apostles had received Christ's teachings directly from him and had witnessed his Resurrection. The Holy Spirit transformed them into courageous evangelists at Pentecost. They had the master plan, but now they had to learn how to apply it to hundreds of new and unexpected situations. They needed to learn how to go from principles to practice.

They came to understand many things only after the passage of time. In the first enthusiastic years of the Christian mission, they fully anticipated that Jesus would come back in their lifetimes to establish the kingdom of heaven on earth.

But as time passed they realized that this was not to be. They were never to know the exact time anyway. Eventually, the hope for an imminent parousia receded into the background, especially when a host of other pastoral issues occupied their attention.

Since the letters to the Thessalonians are probably the first New Testament writings, reflecting the initial growing pains of the infant Church, we can see in them the details of the process of growth. The excitability about the parousia yields to the sobering prospect of an apostasy and the rise of the "man of lawlessness." A few years later they would receive copies of Paul's first letter to the Corinthians. In chapter fifteen they would be disabused of a fanciful, literal description of the resurrection of the dead and instead be confronted by the "mystery" of the event.

Paul had known the uses of apocalyptic talk, but afterwards he also sensed its shortcomings. People must appreciate the depth of the teaching about resurrection and the Second Coming and be willing to let go of concrete images which might stall them in superficial glimpses of a gift from God that will be grander than anything they might imagine.

HOW DOES THIS HELP US TO DEAL WITH THE RAPTURE?

First of all, I think that Paul's pastoral teaching evolved from a childlike picture of the parousia to a sterner and more realistic view that included the apostasy and the antichrist. But he went further in his dealing with Corinth and elevated the teaching to its valued place as a mystery of salvation. In his first two responses he was short and to the point, addressing a pastoral issue in a few sentences and moving on to more expansive catechesis of other matters.

He did not build the parousia or the apostasy and antichrist into a full-blooded analysis of how these matters would be spelled out in real life. He painted no purple prose descriptions of disappearances, hysteria, or mass meetings of distraught people. Actually, he was amazingly matter of fact about it all, plainly outlining what would occur. The parousia would be a beautiful event that confirmed people's faith. The apostasy and antichrist would be visible signs of the "evil one" (Satan) ever attempting to test the believers and draw them into disbelief. That's it.

On the other hand, contrast Paul's third stage of thinking about the resurrection of the body in 1 Corinthians 15. He has obviously had more time to think about the matter and senses he must help his parishioners be more sensitive to the mystery of faith with which they were really dealing. Here he uses less apocalytpic imagery, though the sound of the last trumpet remains, and instead employs metaphors.

He asks us to think of the transformation in terms of a seed and a plant. The plant is the fullness of the seed though it does not look like a seed. Yet the identity remains throughout the process. Paul has taken the mystery of growth and transformation, seen in the agricultural order, and used it as a way to appreciate what happens in the resurrection of the dead at the parousia.

Now let us apply this to the current teachings of millennialists about the rapture and its attendant events. They take Paul's picture of the parousia and blow it up into a literal, physical picture. They add numerous novelistic details full of mysterious disappearances, traffic jams, passenger planes abandoned in midair, and other fanciful vignettes: A surgeon is moving a scalpel along the chest of a patient and she disappears. A funeral director is smoothing the suit of a corpse and it vanishes. A mother shopping at the supermarket takes a box of cornflakes off the shelf and looks horrified at the shopping cart. Her little girl is missing. Only her colorful dress and shoes remain. And so on. The best I can say is that this is a tribute to the writer's imagination. But it has none of the grace of hesitation nor the simplicity of Paul's straightfoward original words about the parousia, which contains no sense of horror or hysteria.

Second, the contemporary millennialists linger on the apostasy and the antichrist with great relish, creating lengthy descriptions of the antichrist and listing a catalog of the sins of modern apostates. At times the anecdotes and reports almost have a tabloid luridness about them. Some of the writing sounds like a rerun of Stephen King's horror stories. Dozens of books and thousands of pages attempt to take Paul's few verses about the antichrist and the apostasy and blow them up into narratives sometimes as long *as Gone With the Wind.*

I do not question the sincerity of these believers. I have to give them credit for taking the parousia seriously. I may not concur with the way they want to talk about it, but I must commend them for never forgetting the truth of the parousia nor ignoring its dynamic usage for Christians. But I believe they would be better served by imitating Paul's own evolution from picturesqueness to mystery.

I can feel as put out by modern apostasy as anyone, but I see little value in creating chronicles of decay. This is not only depressing but also self-defeating. And I believe it sometimes descends merely into gossip. The sins of others may be interesting, but our business is salvation, forgiveness, and charity.

In another part of this book I will present some thoughts about how to interpret the Bible and the prophetic writings in it. Catholics begin with the Church, not the Bible. We certainly believe that Scripture is the Word of God, but we also insist that the books of the New Testament came into existence after the Church whose members wrote the Scriptures. Catholics believe that we need the authority of the Magisterium to help us determine the meaning of the Bible, but let us return to this later.

I do not dispute the energetic attention which millennialists thrust upon us to open our hearts to the parousia. But I refuse the products of overheated imagination that its adherents would demand of me. The example of Paul might be characterized as "less is more." Less heat and more light is what I would suggest. I am grateful for the attention which advocates of the rapture compel me to see. But I very soon languish when confronted with a flurry of anecdotes, news stories, details, political comments, and cultural analysis that is torturously fabricated to prove the point.

It all sounds less like a mystery of faith and more like a kind of spiritual science fiction. (I do not discount religious science fiction of the kind practiced by C.S. Lewis in his wonderful works such as *Perelandra*.) I surely believe in the parousia, affirming it every Sunday in the Nicene Creed. I also believe that the tribulations which precede the end of time will include the apostasy and the antichrist, but I'm not convinced that the rapture adherents have found either a proper way to talk about these mysteries, let alone a convincing argument for believing that the end is actually now about to happen.

I am more inclined to stay with the simplicity of Paul and his quiet evolution. Its does not distract me from the mysteries about the end time. Rather it calls me to dwell on them in prayer and silence, part of my yearly advent waiting for the coming of my Savior. I am taught by this that I must be always ready. That is why Thessalonians contains that best of all spiritual advice:

"Pray without ceasing" (1 Thes 5:17).

CHAPTER FOUR:

HAVE DANIEL'S SEVENTY WEEKS OF YEARS ARRIVED?

The story is told that the angels came to God and asked, "When are the High Holy Days this year?"

"Why are you asking me?" God replied. "Let us go to earth and ask.

"Whenever they say it's the Day of Judgment, I will appear in court."

— Based on Midrash Rabbah, Deuteronomy 2:14-15

On October 22, 1844, fifty thousand American Christians scanned the skies. They believed this was the day the world would end. William Miller, a lay preacher and farmer in Low Hampton, New York, was responsible for this expectation. His Protestant faith motivated him to study the Bible so energetically that he would be able to defend it against any challenge against its teachings.

His Scripture study led him to conclude that God had revealed a timetable for knowing the date for the end of time. He attributed his enlightenment to the Book of Daniel, chapter eight. Daniel had asked God how long the Temple would be defiled by the desolating sin of enshrining a pagan god over the altar. God replied, "For two thousand three hundred evenings and mornings. Then the sanctuary will be purified."

Bill Miller saw in these words a timetable for the end of the world. He interpreted the "purification of the sanctuary" to mean a fire which would consume the world at the end of time. He determined that the biblical word" days" here actually meant years. Granting this, the Book of Daniel was predicting that the world would end in 2,300 years. Miller examined other Scripture passages and concluded that the countdown began in 457 B.C. This calculation allowed him to say the end of time would occur in 1843.

Next he searched for signs of the end time in his own world. Nations were preparing for war. He believed he observed phenomena in the skies that supported his prophecy. For a long time Miller kept these considerations to himself, confiding them only to a few friends and neighbors. But by 1831, the public heard about his predictions. A church invited him to speak on the issue. This was the beginning of several years of lecturing widely and sharing his vision of the end.

By 1842, with only a year left for the end, Miller attracted thousands to his camp meetings where he and other preachers urged people to accept Christ while there was still time. His listeners were not worried about all this because they would be "raptured" and saved from the calamities of world catastrophe. They sang:

> The earth and all the works therein
> Dissolve by raging fires destroyed.
> While we survey the awful scene
> And mount above the fiery void.

Miller believed the Lord would come between March 21, 1843, and March 21, 1844. His followers wanted a more exact date. Somehow people came to believe the end would come on April 23, 1843, a week after Easter. Miller did not approve the date. Nothing happened. Now it was thought there were still eleven months to go. With mounting excitement they awaited March 21, 1844. The news had spread throughout America and some foreign countries. Alas, when the sun arose on March 22, 1844, Miller and his followers were disappointed. The end had not come.

One of his disciples, Samuel Snow, came to the rescue. He argued that Miller had picked the wrong month. The Day of the Lord would be October 22. A few people quit their jobs (like the Thessalonians). A few paid off debts and others sold their worldly goods. Most of them waited quietly and prayerfully for Christ's return. Again they were disappointed.

Critics laughed and described them as crazed fanatics wearing white robes and trying to fly to heaven. The truth was they were devout people who sincerely, but mistakenly, believed they would see God and be swept to heaven by his grace. Their faith in Christ's return was well-grounded in the Bible, but they forgot the other saying of Jesus that it is foolish to try and determine the day and the hour when it would happen.

They were captivated by the repeated line in Scripture which said that the Day of the Lord would come "soon." But the word "soon" in this context must be understood from the aspect of God's eternity, which is not bound by the urgency of earthly time. A thousand days are but a moment from God's point of view. We are destined to work out our salvation in a sinful world, aided by grace and called to take care of our families, live responsibly, work for justice and peace, and witness the glory of God, whether the Day of the Lord is a few days or a few thousand years away.

THE KING DREAMS OF A STATUE

Despite numerous other efforts to name the date of the end and the consequent disappointments, the strange urge to do so continues. Many of these latter day prophets, like William Miller, have an attachment to the Book of Daniel. They believe that the prophet Daniel has given the most concise overview of the geopolitical situation that will exist prior to the coming of Christ.

How do they come to such a conclusion? They begin with the dream of the statue by King Nebuchadnezzar and its interpretation by Daniel (see Daniel 2). The statue had a gold head, silver arms and chest, a bronze belly and thighs, iron legs, and feet of clay (mixed with some iron). A rock came and crushed the statue. The quality of the materials in the statue declined from head to toe, but its power increased the further down it went. Bronze is tougher than gold.

Daniel told the king that the four parts of the statue represent the four great powers of history. While Daniel only identified the gold head with Babylon and simply said the other parts of the body represented future empires, scholars have supplied the names of the others.

The gold head represented Babylon, a nation known for its fondness for gold. Nebuchadnezzar sat on a throne of gold and wanted to make Babylon a city of gold. He had built a statue of gold that stood ninety feet high.

The silver section referred to the empire of the Medes and Persians. The word for silver in Aramaic also means taxes. The Medes and Persians had enforced a well-organized system of taxation and wanted the money in silver, unlike the Babylonians who would only settle for gold. (A different scheme, promoted by some scholars, relates that silver only refers to the Medes and the iron stands for the Persians. Here I follow a more traditional interpretation.)

The bronze belly and thighs stand for the Greek Empire. Greek solders wore bronze helmets and breastplates, carried bronze shields, and brandished bronze swords.

The iron legs pointed to the Roman Empire. The iron discipline of the Roman soldiers enabled them to conquer the world. But the feet had some iron mixed in with the clay. This seems to reflect the fact that Rome left local cultures free to be themselves so long as they remained faithful to the Empire — and paid their taxes. As the center weakened these cultures would rebel. The clay would be Rome's vulnerable heel.

Daniel proceeded to say that a rock would come and destroy all these empires. The rock would be fashioned by God, whose divine kingdom would overthrow all those empires. ". . . the God of heaven will set up a kingdom that shall never be destroyed or delivered to another people; rather, it shall break in pieces all these kingdoms and put an end to them, and it shall stand forever. That is the meaning of the stone you saw hewn from the mountain without a hand being put to it, which broke in pieces the tile [clay], iron, bronze, silver, and gold" (Dn 2:44-45).

What does the stone which smashes the statue mean? It is a stone not made by human hands. It becomes a mountain that embraces the world. It evokes the biblical theme of the "cornerstone." "The stone which the builders rejected/ has become the cornerstone. / By the Lord has this been done; / it is wonderful in our eyes" (Ps 118:22-23).

Who is this cornerstone?

In defending his healing of the lame man, Peter tells the Sanhedrin that the cornerstone is Jesus Christ. ". . . it was in the name of Jesus Christ the Nazorean whom you crucified, whom God raised from the dead; in his name this man stands before you healed. He is 'the stone rejected by you the builders, which has become the cornerstone' " (Acts 4:10-11). Paul says the same thing in Romans 9:33.

The dream of the stone says that God will make a rock that will overthrow four great empires. The New Testament clarifies that image by teaching that the stone is Christ and his everlasting kingdom. Christ's coming during the days of the Roman Empire established the Christian Church which witnessed the Kingdom of Heaven and lived to see the fall of the Empire.

Millenialists, however, carry this image further. The legs of iron and feet of clay will *reappear* in a renewed coalition of peoples and nations similar to the Roman Empire as it existed centuries before.

DANIEL'S VISION OF THE FOUR BEASTS

But there is more in Daniel.

Daniel had a vision of four beasts (read Daniel 7:1-28). These beasts are another version of the four empires embodied by the statue. The lion is Babylon. The bear is the empire of the Medes and Persians. The leopard is the Greek Empire. The fourth beast is so unusual it cannot be recognized — or so horrible it is beyond naming. This beast is the Roman Empire.

Out of the fourth beast ten horns emerge. Then an eleventh horn comes along and three of the ten horns give it allegiance. This eleventh horn persecutes the saints. Then the Ancient of Days (God) will come and pronounce judgment in favor of the saints. What does this mean?

Millennialists claim there are two phases of the Roman Empire. The appearance of the unnamed beast refers to the original Roman Empire of history. The ten horns refer to a second phase, another empire like that of Rome — and in our own day. The ten horns entail a coalition of countries with political and economic ties. These countries will be within the boundaries of the original Roman Empire.

The arrival of the "eleventh horn" is the emergence of the antichrist. What will he do? He will speak against God. He will oppress God's saints. He will change natural, civil, and moral laws in accord with his own self-declared divinity. How long will this persecution last? Three and one-half years (see Daniel 7:25, 12:7).

However, God will come in judgment to strip the beast of his power (see Daniel 7:26-27). God will convene a court and set up his kingdom. "Then the kingship and dominion and majesty / of all the kingdoms under the heavens / shall be given to the holy people of the Most High" (Dn 7:27).

The dream of the statue and the vision of the four beasts set the stage for the third component in the millennial view of the end time — the timetable of the seventy weeks of years.

THE SEVENTY WEEKS OF YEARS

It is important to review the millennialist understanding of Daniel's dealing with the dream of the statue and the vision of the four beasts before looking at the third piece of the puzzle — the meaning of the seventy weeks of years — or 490 years (see Daniel 9:24-27).

Daniel had been praying for light about the future of his

people and the meaning of another vision described in chapter eight. God answered his prayer and sent the angel Gabriel, who spoke to him about the rebuilding of the Temple and the city of Jerusalem. An anointed king will come after this, but will be "cut off." Finally, a "destroyer" will come. All this will happen over a period of seventy weeks of years.

Millennialists have devised an ingenious interpretation of this text. They apply it to what they see as three phases of Jewish history which correspond to seven weeks of years (forty-nine years; Dn 9:25), sixty-two weeks of years (434 years; Dn 9:25) and one week of years (seven years; Dn 9:27). The total is seventy weeks of years or 490 years. God's plan for them includes six matters:

1. To finish transgressions
2. To put an end to sin
3. To atone for evil

(These three issues will be achieved in Christ's First Coming as Redeemer.)

4. To bring eternal grace
5. To close the pages of history
6. To anoint the Holy Temple

(These three events will be accomplished in Christ's Second Coming.)

Daniel 9:24 states that a decree will be issued to rebuild the temple and the city of Jerusalem — and after this the anointed one will come. What decree is this? Cyrus had decreed the rebuilding of the temple in 538 B.C. Artaxerxes decreed the restoration of Jewish worship in 458 B.C. Again Artaxerxes decreed the rebuilding of Jerusalem in 445 B.C. This last decree occurs sixty-nine weeks of years before the anointed one is "cut off," meaning crucified at Calvary. Hence the third decree must be the one to which Daniel referred.

Now there is one week of years left to the prophecy. When will that happen? When will the seventieth week of years occur? This is when the antichrist is supposed to appear. "And the people of a leader who will come / shall destroy the sanctuary. . . . For one week he shall make a firm compact" (Dn 9:26-27).

If the last week of years had come right after the previous sixty-nine weeks, the antichrist would have appeared right after the death and resurrection of Christ. But from what we know about history that did not happen. So what can we say about the prediction? Here the millennialists take a breathtaking leap. I have already referred to this as the "postponement theory" of history in which God's final plans are only operative when Israel has a national identity. Dr. Ed Dobson, pastor of the three-thousand-member Calvary Church in Grand Rapids, Michigan, belongs to this tradition. He writes:

> "I suggest that between the sixty-ninth and seventieth weeks there is *a parenthesis in human history* [emphasis mine]. This period of time is not dealt with in the prophecy. It is in fact the time period in which we are now living — the Church age" (*The End*, Zondervan, Grand Rapids, 1997, pp.74-75).

How does he account for this "parenthesis?" He argues that St. Paul writes about the Church as a "mystery" that was not made known to people in other generations. It needed New Testament revelation. So God would have hidden this mystery from Daniel, who could not know there would be an age of the Church in between the sixty-ninth week of years and the seventieth.

Let us now come to the last week of years. What should we anticipate? Daniel 9:26-27 predicts the reappearance of an anti-God person (the antichrist in later thinking) who will persecute the saints and set up the abomination of desolation in the temple for three and a half years. The New Testament recaps this prophecy in Matthew 24:15-21, 30-31; and Revelation 13:5-8.

Reverend Dobson relates concisely the millenialist view of the last seven years of history:

> At the end of time the Messiah will return again to the nation of Israel and the city of Jerusalem. But just before he comes, the antichrist will come onto the scene and form a coalition with Israel for seven years. In the middle of the seventh year she will break that covenant. He will bring about the abomination of desolation and then *it* happens! God will close the envelope of history as we know it. He will seal the vision and say to the saints, "Folks, it's time to go back down." In glory, majesty and power, Christ will return" (Dobson, *The End*, p. 78).

Like many other millennialists, Dobson follows the theme of the re-appearance of the Roman Empire (remember the iron legs and feet of clay of the statue and the fourth unnamed beast). It will re-incarnate in the ten states of the European Union that are within the boundaries of the ancient empire. A clever leader (the "eleventh horn") will take over this political entity and emerge as the antichrist, and so on.

WHAT'S A CATHOLIC TO THINK OF SEVENTY WEEKS OF YEARS?

If nothing else, we must credit millennialists with lively imaginations. Of course we should also acknowledge their fervent faith and their ability to make the rest of us take seriously the doctrine of the Second Coming of Christ which we recite each Sunday in the Nicene Creed. But our Catholic faith does not require the kind of Scripture interpretation that the millennialists would offer us.

63

By now you can see the assumptions we would have to make to believe the millennial scenarios. We would need to accept the "postponement theory" (or parenthesis model) of history which asks us to think that biblical prophecy about the parousia operates only while Israel is a nation. Anything that happens from A.D. 70 to 1948 is left aside; otherwise the model doesn't work.

All I can say is that is an interesting idea, but it has no foundation either in Scripture nor in Church teaching. Why should I believe that the prophetic clock stopped in A.D. 70? To justify a theory? Who said so? What is the authority of the speaker? Here as elsewhere you can see the value of an authoritative Church which has been helping us to understand the Bible for two thousand years.

Never has it taught such a theory — quite the opposite. The Church incorporates biblical prophecy into the entire history of salvation and its application to Church history. The Holy Spirit hasn't taken a holiday. The Spirit abides with the Church as a Teacher and Guide to the meaning of prophecy.

Second, we would have to treat numbers in Scripture literally. The threes, sevens, twelves, forties, and thousands would all be exactly what they say. But Scripture is not a mathematically precise book. The numbers in the Bible give us an order of magnitude. One of the best examples of the symbolic meaning of biblical numbers is given by Jesus himself, who invites us to forgive "seventy times seven" (Mt 18:22). He did not mean we must at least forgive 490 times and then it's ok not to forgive. The idea is very clear. We must forgive always.

Numbers in the Bible often have a symbolic meaning. *One* means primacy and excellence. *Four* refers to universality, as in the four corners of the earth. *Six* stands for imperfection. Hence the beast of the Apocalypse is 666, the most imperfect of beings. But *seven* means perfection, fullness, totality as in the seven days of creation. *Twelve* is a popular number in the Bible, obviously referring to the tribes of Israel and the apostles, but also in many symbolic ways. A *thousand* means a large multitude or a long time, not necessarily an exact one thousand of whatever.

Numbers need to be taken in context. Sometimes they are symbolic and sometimes they are numerically what they say. The seventy weeks of years in Daniel are more obviously a symbolic number. The millennialists need to find arbitrary starting dates and a parenthesis idea of history to make their scenario work. This simply proves the numbers are not meant to be taken literally.

Third, we are once again asked to accept the idea that the Roman Empire will re-appear in a coalition of ten European nations. It shouldn't take much for you to see how hard this will be to apply to Europe's fluid political climate. The expansion of NATO and the emergence of other European nations eager to join the Union will require a lot of geopolitical juggling to make it match the ten nation theory (based on Daniel's ten horns).

Biblical prophets read the signs of their own history in the light of God's revealed covenant to try and discern God's will for their people. They were inspired by the Holy Spirit; as our Creed says, the Holy Spirit spoke through the prophets. But the Spirit was not giving them accurate video displays of the future nor mathematical timetables for the Day of the Lord. Daniel did not say that Persia, Greece, and Rome were represented by the Statue and the Beasts. He just spoke generally about empires hostile to God.

Other prophets foretold a messiah but mentioned no timetable. People thought their writings referred to a political and royal messiah like King David. Only when the Word becomes flesh do many of the prophecies become clear, such as Isaiah's stirring chapter fifty-three about the suffering servant and its realization in Christ's passion.

Prophets are not fortunetellers. They are people of faith who respond to the Spirit and communicate the mysteries of salvation. Only in the fullness of time do their words come true and the meaning embedded in their sayings become evident. They also walked in the darkness of faith as well as in the light of revelation. There was nothing simple about the prophets. Their complex lives and messages should not be reduced to easy formulas.

The Holy Spirit who spoke through Daniel and the other prophets also rests in the heart of our Church, teaching, guiding, and enlightening God's people. On issues of doctrine the Spirit protects the truth of revelation through the Church's Magisterium.

What shall we say then about Daniel's seventy weeks of years? The Spirit moved Daniel to teach the doctrine of God's mercy and religious hope for Israel. Hostile empires will try to destroy God's people, but they will not succeed. A Savior will come and overcome the anti-god (antichrist) and deliver the saints from persecution and into glory with the Ancient One. This will happen over a long period of time — the symbolic seventy weeks of years, a way of talking about the whole subsequent history of salvation, not excluding the time between A.D. 70 and 1948. Did Daniel know all the details? No. Do we know all the details? No. We live in both light and mystery.

It's a humbling calling.

CHAPTER FIVE:

JOACHIM OF FIORE VS. AUGUSTINE AND EZEKIEL

"Brother Peter, what do you think of the doctrine of Abbot Joachim?"

"I think it's about as useful as the fifth wheel on a four-wheel cart."

— A Legend

In 1167, a young chancery official from Calabria made a pilgrimage to the Holy Land. His name was Joachim and he possessed the soul of an idealistic seeker. He yearned to be perfect. He spent some time with a group of desert hermits. On Mount Thabor, traditional site of Christ's transfiguration, Joachim received a vision of God the Father. He would later have visions of the Son and the Holy Spirit. After a Lenten retreat in Jerusalem, he returned home. His pilgrimage proved to be a conversion experience for him and a defining event of his life.

He resigned his chancery post and joined a Cistercian monastery in Corrazzo. Ordained a priest in 1168, he was elected Abbot ten years later. But even this austere and inspiring order was not perfect enough for him. At the age of fifty, he left his abbey and went to Fiore, where he intended to create the most perfect form of monastic life. He would always be known thereafter as Joachim of Fiore.

He devoted these years in solitude to writing out his interpretations of history. Partly because of his visions and partly through his study of the Bible, he adopted a worldview which saw history as divided into three ages.

The first was the Age of the Father in Old Testament times. It was marked by fear and slavish obedience. It was symbolized by married people and the elderly.

The second was Age of the Son in the New Testament period and Church history up to his own day. Faith and filial obedience characterized this period. Clergy and young people exemplified its spirit.

He then foresaw the Age of the Spirit, which he claimed would begin in 1260. Love and freedom would be its hallmarks. Monks and infants would be its emblems.

He pictured a rosy future in this third age. The visible Church would be replaced by an invisible Church of the Spirit. Bishops and clergy would receive new roles in this spiritualized Church. Contemplative life would replace active ministry. Jews would become Christians. The eastern and western churches would unite.

There would be no more war. Love would rule every heart. All people would live the beatitudes until the end of time. The eternal good news proclaimed by the angel in Apocalypse 14:6 would become a reality. "Then I saw another angel flying high overhead, with everlasting good news. . . ." In other words, the Spirit would create a Christian utopia on earth.

Joachim enjoyed playing the prophet and won widespread attention and acceptance. How did he escape censure from the Church of his day? He was a man of great personal charm. He was on speaking terms with three popes and other major Church leaders. His quest for spiritual ideals was admired. He lived a virtuous life. He always humbly submitted his writings for Church approval. (In fact, his teaching on the Trinity as a loose federation of three persons would be rejected by the fourth Lateran Council in 1215.) In a time of fervent ecclesiastical reform, he seemed to be perfectly in tune with its spirit.

Thomas Aquinas did not agree with Joachim's "Third Age of the Spirit." For Aquinas, there are three stages in our history of salvation: the Old Testament, the New Testament, and Heaven. The New Testament historical period will last as long as this world does. Aquinas makes clear that Jesus is the center of history and that he promised and gave the Holy Spirit already at the beginning of Christianity.

The risen Christ said to the apostles, ". . . in a few days you will be baptized with the holy Spirit" (Acts 1:5). The giving of the Spirit at Pentecost in Acts chapter two demonstrates that Christ's promise was fulfilled. We already have the Spirit, and in this sense we are already in the age of the Spirit. Thomas doesn't waste words about Joachim, "And this is sufficient to expose the emptiness of anyone else who says that we should look forward to some new time of the Holy Spirit" (*Summa*, I-IIae, 106, 4).

Thomas delivers a second punch by noting that the Spirit taught the apostles all the truth they needed to be saved and to share with others about salvation. The Spirit let them know what should be believed and done to be saved. However, the Spirit did not teach them everything that would happen in the future. This was apparently none of their business.

" 'Lord, are you at this time going to restore the kingdom to Israel?' He answered them, 'It is not for you to know the times or seasons that the Father has established by his own authority' " (Acts 1:6-7). Aquinas is saying that the end of history is a mystery known only to the Father and will happen in God's own good time.

After his death, Joachim's writings were adopted by dissenters and heretics who freely distorted his teachings and mixed them into their own millennial versions of history. His ideas about the possibilities of an earthly millennium were also adopted by secular thinkers and, indirectly, supported the modern theories of the thousand years of Aryan supremacy and the "workers' paradise."

Joachim's dreams appealed to many Protestant reformers who saw their new churches as belonging to his Age of the Spirit. No longer would a visible church be needed, with its priests, sacraments, and hierarchy. There would be a spiritual church centered around the priesthood of all believers.

The fact that his prediction about the arrival of the Age of the Spirit in 1260 failed to occur bothered no one. Then as now, true millennial believers just changed the dates, always finding reasons why the prophesied time was not exactly right.

I share Joachim of Fiore's story with you in this book because he sowed into western history the recurring dream of an earthly millennium. For some this would be a Christian utopia, for others a secular one. He translated his personal idealism into the myth of progress. History is the place where matters will get better and better. Joachim predicted this would be caused by an intervention of the Spirit. His secular heirs claim that organized human effort and a clear sense of purpose will make it happen.

He predicted that catastrophes and tribulations would be crises that mark the end of the old order and the arrival of the perfect one. Effectively, he made himself a rival alternative to Augustine's vision of history. Whether we are aware of Joachim or not, we are heirs to the stream of historical interpretation which he invented in the twelfth century.

The millennial impulse has always attracted those who weep for their own times. It enchants the disenchanted. It mesmerizes people who are painfully dissatisfied with the failures and tragedies of their own culture. They are too impatient to wait for heaven hereafter — they want a heaven on earth. They will not settle for a slow, incremental improvement of people and structures. Something more dramatic and revolutionary is needed. A theory of history that seems to promise this will have passionate disciples. I suggest that we have a better model for interpreting the future in the teachings of St. Augustine.

AUGUSTINE: "TWO LOVES BUILT TWO CITIES"

"Two loves built two cities," wrote St. Augustine in his *City of God*. The love of God built the City of God. The love of this world built the City of Man. Long before Joachim, Augustine worked out an understanding of how history works. He had no taste for millennial fantasies, even though he lived in cataclysmic times.

In his old age, Augustine lived to see his beloved classical culture crumble before the barbarians. He also realized that the Church he loved with all his heart would face enormous problems of survival as all the structures of society collapsed. When he was on his deathbed, the Vandals were at the city wall.

If anyone ever faced a secular end of "a" world it was Augustine and his contemporaries. In a very real sense, Augustine knew what an end of a world felt like. Yet he never concluded it was the end of "the" world.

The crisis did not motivate him to predict the arrival of the Age of the Spirit or any other kind of millennial prospect. He had every reason to be alarmist, but he wasn't. The tribulations of the Apocalypse looked very real to him when he saw the barbarians at the gates. But he had no inclination to take them as signs of the end of history. He took seriously the words of Jesus: "But of that day and hour no one knows . . . but the father alone" (Mt 24:36).

Augustine was always hesitant to make sharp comparisons between biblical scenes and actual events of his own history. He was more fascinated by the inner dramas of love between God and an immense variety of individuals — a series of millions of mystery plays that were the true driving force of history. The drama was interior, but was acted out in time, in history itself.

The facts of history that preoccupy historians were not Augustine's real interest. Eventually, he added a great number of historical events to his *City of God*, but that was due to demands from his readers for "evidence" for his theories. Stubbornly, he returned again and again to his "inner drama" principle.

He rejected any attempt to correlate the events of his own time with the history of the *City of God*. It did not matter to him whether the news stories of the day were favorable or unfavorable to Christianity. He did not try to make them fit some scheme of the end of time. He considered it useless to have an apocalyptic mentality that used biblical or secular methods to predict the end of history.

I highlight this for you because today's millenarians love to take biblical prophecies and use them for geo-political analysis. They speak of the New World Order, the state of Israel, and other political developments as fulfillment of biblical prophecy. I shall deal with this in another chapter. Nothing could be further from Augustine's method for interpreting history.

His theory of history included both earthly and spiritual progress. Never, however, was this a kind of determinism such as we saw in twentieth-century millennia tried by the Nazis and the Communists. Earthly progress in culture and civilization could be identified in the histories of Greece and Rome. The divine progress could not be seen, other than in the general revealed truths in Scripture. There the prophets and apostles identified the progress of the divine plan of salvation that was fulfilled in Christ and continues, under the Spirit, in the Church and the sacraments.

Augustine was fascinated by the mystery of the eternal God working somehow within the confines of time. He had examined time and its effect on us in his *Confessions.* Since history and memory go together, he needed to examine his own memory life. He looked at his own soul, marveling at the enormous range of his memory — even buried memories.

> The power of memory is prodigious, my God.
> It is a vast immeasurable sanctuary. . . . My
> memory contains my feelings, not in the same
> way as they are present to the mind when it
> experiences them, but in a quite different way
> that is in keeping with the special powers of
> the memory. For even when I am unhappy I
> can remember times when I was cheerful and
> when I am cheerful I can remember past un-
> happiness. I can recall past fears and yet not

feel afraid, and when I remember that I once wanted something I can do so without wishing to have it now (*Confessions*, Book X, 8, 14).

At the same time, he noted his soul stretching toward the future. It is impossible not to wonder about what lies ahead. Just like us, he lived between memory and expectation.

This insight into his inner life caused Augustine to feel keenly the problem of being a fallen soul. He sensed its heaviness as it dragged him toward things that are not of God. It left him empty and unsatisfied. The history of his soul would be a tragedy without the grace of Christ the Savior. Divine grace liberated him from the gravitational pull to that which separated him from God.

Grace, the experience of divine love, pitched him into an ascent to God. The Lord moved him into a different field of gravity. Love raised him up. Perhaps even the sophisticated Augustine would appreciate the old American country-and-western hymn, "Love lifted me. Love lifted me. When I was down and out, Love lifted me."

For Augustine, history (or time) marks the distance that separates the creature and the creator. But we have no choice but to live in time. It is in and through history that we make the decisions that will open us to salvation. History is the arena where the victory of the "Athlete of Christ" will happen or where damnation will occur. Augustine never asked his parishioners to flee from time. It is only in history that conversion and spiritual and human fulfillment takes place.

As a preacher during tough times, Augustine treated his people as real human beings facing a host of difficulties. He was well aware of the tenacity of the links that bind his Christians to the world. His parishioners are indeed pilgrims on their way to heaven — at least that is what he hoped. They are temporary residents in history. He and they together have an intimate dependence on life around them. He wanted to help them achieve some good and avoid some greater evil.

Augustine's *City of God* did not recommend a flight from the world. He worried about their day to day activities in this common mortal life. The people in his sermons are sturdy sinners who enjoy what they do. He realized their capacity for love.

> I do not criticize you, even if this life is what you love. . . . You can love this life all you want, as long as you know what to choose. Let us therefore be able to choose our life, if we are capable of loving it (*Sermon* 297, 4).

No matter how difficult the times were, they should not run away from life. They should do something more demanding. They ought to maintain a firm and balanced perspective on the whole range of loves of which they were capable in their present state. In the context of our discussion about the millennium, this would mean we would be wiser to "stick to our knitting" in turbulent times rather than surrender ourselves to pipe dreams about a millennium. Escapism seems like fun, but it is a useless and dangerous passion.

Augustine knew that his people existed on a scale from faithful to almost faithless. He realized they experienced this as a blend, an inseparable mixture. They needed to live in two cities at once, that of God and of the world. As their pastor, he had to help them keep their feet on the earth and their hearts in heaven and not be broken by the tension. He energized their identity in this manner and protected them both from millenarian fantasies and from a surrender to the world alone. His soul was closer to the biblical Ezekiel than it would have been to the medieval Joachim. Augustine was not as gloomy as Ezekiel, but he could recognize in the prophet a kindred spirit struggling with historical breakdown and arriving at a similar faith solution to a historical challenge.

THE EZEKIEL FACTOR

We have looked at the story of a monk who predicted a millennial Age of the Spirit and the view of a bishop who actually lived in tumultuous times but refused to see them as a prelude to a millennium. Now let us go back to the story of a biblical prophet who spent most of his life in exile and who used apocalyptic language to mobilize the faith of his people.

In the year 587 B.C., Babylon was the world's superpower. Its armies overwhelmed Jerusalem and deported thousands of Jews. This was the beginning of the Babylonian captivity of the Jewish people, an exile that lasted about seventy years. Among its exiles was the thirty-year-old priest named Ezekiel. He had seen the end of his world as he knew it. A powerful enemy had forced him to live in a strange culture. Like his compatriots, he was a shaken man.

One day, as he sat on the bank of the river Chebar, he received an extraordinary vision. He saw the sky open and the clouds flashing with lightning. Four angels appeared each bearing a different image and representing qualities popular in the biblical mind. One had the face of an ox, the strongest of creatures. Another wore the face of the noblest animal, the lion. The third bore the image of an eagle, the fiercest of birds. The fourth presented the face of a human, the wisest of creatures.

The scene was full of movement caused by fiery wheels that spun through the air and shimmered with flaming torches. He heard the roar of rushing waters that sounded to him like the voice of God. Then a sapphire throne appeared and on it sat God himself. A rainbow framed the throne and God's glory flowed from his presence. The description reads like contemporary science fiction, as though a rumbling, brilliant, giant spacecraft sparkling with diamonds had intruded into our orbit.

Terrified with fear, Ezekiel prostrated himself on the ground. But God was not interested in frightening the young man. The Lord ordered him to stand up because he had a mission for this earnest young priest. God called Ezekiel to be a prophet to the exiles. The message he would bring was symbolized by the eating of a scroll, in other words totally assimilating the Word of the Lord. Surprisingly, Ezekiel found the scroll to be as sweet as honey.

And so he embarked on a career of prophecy, alternately speaking to his people about their loss of faith and calling them to conversion. He encouraged them to hope in God, who would create a new covenant in the future.

God had given Ezekiel a very demanding call. The Jewish community was facing the greatest religious crisis in its history since the slave days in Egypt. Their covenant with God and their daily religious life had been supported by a social, political, and economic culture in the Holy Land. Now they were marooned in a Babylonian world that was indifferent and even hostile to their faith. They were a second-class minority people and religion. Economically, they were not doing too badly. They were able to support their families and even acquire a mild prosperity. They were not oppressed, though they were depressed at times:

> By the streams of Babylon
> we sat and wept
> when we remembered Zion. . . .
> And our despoilers urged us to be joyous:
> "Sing for us the songs of Zion!"
> How could we sing the song of the Lord
> in a foreign land?   (Ps 137:1, 3-4).

They had no temple, no priesthood, no religious culture to support and enliven their faith. With the passing of years they would be tempted to assimilated into Babylonian culture and eventually forget the God of their ancestors. Gradually a number of them would accede to the new situation and let go of their faith.

They had already undergone the crisis of deportation, establishing themselves in a new land and trying to make a living. Now a more subtle crisis faces them, the possible abandonment of their religion. God calls Ezekiel to shape the people into a "religious community in exile."

Since they have no temple, they will need some kind of religious assembly places. Thus emerged synagogues, or meeting houses. Here they could pray together, meditate on the Bible, and hear sermons that would keep them in touch with God and resolve to keep the covenant and commandments. These gatherings would be supplemented by religious family customs in their homes. The combination of sacred home and sacred meeting place helped them maintain their religious and cultural identity.

Ezekiel decided that crisis language would be the most effective for spurring the faith of his listeners. Another name for such language is apocalyptic talk. With its dramatic imagery of storms, fire, blood, famine, and descriptions of God in glory (taken from his visions), he issued a stream of wake-up calls to his people.

Little by little he made them into a coherent culture within a culture. He urged Jewish religious identity upon them, so successfully that he became known as the "Father of Judaism." In his parable of the Dry Bones (Ez 37), he described them as a field of skeletons which will rise again to new life in their own land by the power of God.

His final eight chapters are an inspiring vision of the Israel of the future, purified of past evils and established again under the firm rule of the Lord. God will bring about this restoration. *This would not be a millennium so much as a fresh start*. He argued that they were in exile because they had lost a sense of the holiness of God. "What is holy to me you have spurned, and my sabbaths you have desecrated. . . . I have relented because of my holy name which the house of Israel profaned among the nations where they came"(Ez 22:8, 36:21).

Ezekiel proposed that in the future the sacred space of God, the temple, would be separated from anything profane. His plans for the rebuilding of the temple were like the precautions taken in a hospital operating room to keep it sanitary. The royal palace was on the old temple's grounds as were the kings' tombs. Uncircumcised janitors were hired to care for the place. Unlawful practices were tolerated within the ancient temple's precincts.

No longer would that happen. In minute detail he pictured the new temple. Walled courtyards would surround the temple area. Laity would worship in the outer court, while priests would minister in the inner court. His attention to detail, even to every aspect of temple furnishings, showed his consuming desire to keep the holy place from anything profane. He composed rules for such things as the offering of animals and vegetables, the materials and tailoring of the priestly vestments, and the opening and closing of gates.

He was aware of dealing with human error and mistakes and prescribed purification rituals to take care of this. His attention was focused on public worship because he wanted a friendly relationship between God and the whole people. He had little interest in private sacrifices *per se*, assuming that a proper public order would keep the private world intact. He introduced a solemnity to public worship that left little room for spontaneity. He hoped to drive home a sense of awe for the majesty and holiness of God.

His liturgical reform was radical and lasting. It may have had the weakness of being over-organized, leaving little room for the spontaneous, but his vision put fiber into the national religion. He was a grouchy, sometimes fanatical prophet, but his basic wisdom did instill a sense of responsibility in a thoughtless people. We will always cherish his "legacy of the holy," and in our own times struggle to preserve the sacred in a secular society.

I have told the Ezekiel story because he did what apocalyptic millenarians like to do, that is, analyze history and politics in terms of scriptural prophecy. He is known, along with Daniel, as one of the founders of scriptural apocalypses. Just compare his vision and call to prophecy in Ezekiel chapters one through three with the call of St. John in the Book of Revelation (1:9-20), and with the heavenly liturgy in Revelation 4:1-11.

Like Augustine, he gives an interpretation of history as the arena of God's actions and also the battleground for our spiritual combat. Like Joachim of Fiore, he foresees a glowing future that is almost like a Jewish utopia, an Age of the Spirit. The difference is that Ezekiel does not predict a perfect world. Human error and sinfulness will abide. The best we can do is provide an all-embracing sacred environment to provide the best hope for a faith life. Add to this the purification rites needed to keep bringing people back to religious ideals.

Ezekiel would have Augustine's realistic assessment of the weakness of human beings, but not enough of the bishop's vision of human potential aided by grace. Both were tough-minded, hands-on religious pastors, but Augustine's breadth of insight into the possibilities of love of God and neighbor appear more liberating to me.

I use Ezekiel and Augustine as foils for Joachim because they dealt with apocalyptic times and experiences without becoming utopian or millennial in the dangerous sense. Moreover, the biblical prophet and the Catholic bishop avoid literal applications of Scripture (yes, even a biblical prophet is not a literal interpreter of other parts of Scripture) to historical events, whether the present or the future. They have too much respect for the mystery of God and his interaction with us in time. They have enormous faith in God's plan to save us. They leave the Lord free to choose the time and the place for the new appearances of his gracious salvation.

Augustine and Ezekiel offer us wise options for understanding our history no matter how calamitous it is. We are far better off living by faith and trust in the Lord of history and so attending to the daily demands of life with equanimity, praying, working, loving, and helping those around us to keep their heads about them. That is about as millennial as I would get.

CHAPTER SIX:

WHOSE "FOUR LAST THINGS" SHOULD YOU BELIEVE?

The world is charged with the grandeur of God.
It will flame out, like shining from shook foil.
— Gerard Manley Hopkins

"In 1907 Henry Adams wrote that in the modern world the dynamo had replaced the Virgin as the power that drives history. Were he around today, it is the computer, not the dynamo, which would impress him with its occult powers and emanations of moral force. It enables the mind to ask questions, find answers, stockpile knowledge, and devise plans to move mountains if not worlds.

"An outfit called the Millennium Society has lined up the QE2 to transport 3,000 people, all presumably upbeat, to a huge celebration at the Great Pyramid of Cheops. As Barbara Tuchman put it, people feel 'as if the hand of God were turning a page in human history.' We have a sense of things ending and others beginning.

"First, of course, we are witnessing the end of communism, and beginning to cope with what this will mean for capitalism.

"Second, we are witnessing the end of nationalism as we have known it and beginning to look for new international arrangements.

"And third, we are witnessing the end, or at least the decline, of an age of unbelief and the beginning of what may be a new age of faith" (Henry Grunwald, *Time,* March 30, 1992, p.73).

Apocalypse Chapter 20:1-6

The only place in the Bible that speaks of the millennium (the "thousand days") is in the first six verses of the Apocalypse, or Revelation, chapter twenty. Christians have debated its meaning ever since the days of the early Church. Did St. John predict an actual event that will happen at some future time in history? Or was he speaking symbolically as was so often the case in his Book of Revelation?

One school of thought believes he meant a literal reign of Jesus on earth for a thousand years. From the earliest days of the Church, some Christian writers (Justin, Irenaeus, Tertullian) have understood Apocalypse 20:1-6 as an actual thousand-year reign of Christ. Followers of this interpretation often upset bishops and dioceses in the church of the East so much that many eastern bishops refrained from accepting the Apocalypse as inspired Scripture until the ninth century. As you know, by now there are millions of millenarian Christians today who also think of this in literal terms.

But there is another school of thought that considers the "thousand days" as a symbolic description of the "era of the Church" between Christ's first coming in Galilee until his Second Coming at the end of history.

In the first five chapters of this book I have explored with you millenarian themes which surround the thousand days: the rapture, the antichrist, the tribulations, and ideas about the Second Coming. I now propose to contrast these theories about the last things with the Catholic Church's traditional teachings about our final destinies.

The Four Last Things

In Catholic teaching, the four last things are: death, judgment, heaven, and hell.

In millenarian theory, the four last things are: rapture, tribulation, millennium, Second Coming.

Let us take the millenarian steps and evaluate them from a

Catholic perspective. I would then briefly review with you the four last things of Catholic teaching.

I. RAPTURE
(See 1 Thessalonians 4:16-17.)

Allow me to review what I said earlier about the rapture.

St. Paul wrote his letter to the Thessalonians at a time when Christians believed the Second Coming of Christ would happen very soon. The Thessalonians wanted to know what it would be like. They were eager to see the Jesus they had heard so much about. There were still apostles and disciples alive who had seen Jesus in Galilee and Judea before his death and had beheld him again in his risen state. It was only about seventeen years since the Ascension. St. Paul himself had gazed on the risen Lord in his Damascus vision. When is he coming again? What will the experience be like?

To respond to their questions, Paul used images that fit the mentality of the times. They believed the earth was flat. They thought the sky was like a cake bowl, a solid dome that covered the earth. God had fixed the sun, moon, and stars into this solid dome. Mysterious powers, most likely angels, moved these heavenly lights around, events that accounted for night and day.

Above the dome was the third heaven where lived the Trinity, angels, and saints. (The first heaven was the air between the dome and earth. The second heaven was the dome itself.) It was only natural for Paul to use height and space pictures to envision the Second Coming. If Christ is up there above the starry skies, he must come from there. If we are to be brought into his new kingdom, then we would rise up in the air to meet him and be transported to the heavenly realms above the sky. Millenarians love this picture and speak of it as the rapture, the first of their last four things.

But as time passed no Second Coming was happening. Paul realized that he must revise his thinking. The manifestation of

Christ's glory (called the parousia) in the final days could not be assumed to happen as quickly as he once believed. So in his second letter to the Thessalonians he counseled them to cool their ardor. It was more important for them to observe their daily duties and develop strong Christian lives. They should attend to the work of the Holy Spirit, who was taking them through the processes of sanctification.

Several years later, in writing to the Corinthians, Paul said that indeed one day the "trumpet shall sound and the dead will be raised incorruptible." But now he was far more interested in helping his congregations understand the transformation from death to resurrection. He seemed no longer interested in spectacular ascensions into the air, but rather in the spiritual transfigurations of the bodies of those who would rise with Christ.

Hence Paul's teaching evolved from a simple scene of the just rising in the air to meet Christ, to a more down-to-earth reflection on the daily commitment to sanctification, and to a profound meditation on the resurrection of the body (read 1 Corinthians 15). Of course Paul was not ignoring the Second Coming, for he joyfully spoke of the sounding of the last trumpet that signaled the parousia. Under the guidance of the Spirit, Paul probed the mystery of the Resurrection as well as the mystery of time, for we will not know the precise date of the Second Coming.

Millenarians have zeroed in on Paul's first image of Jesus coming and believers rising in the air to meet him. This is what they call the rapture, and they accept a first-century cosmology (the sky as a dome, etc.) as the way it will happen.

Catholics also see the Thessalonian words as a teaching about Christ's Second Coming. But we remain reserved as to how this will happen. The physical image of bodies rising in the air is at best a way of speaking about the resurrection of the body. Catholics are more at home with Paul in 1 Corinthians chapter fifteen when he says, "Behold I tell you a mystery" (15:51). In using the expression "mystery" Paul moves the discussion through the visible to the invisible. He asks us to treat

84

these truths as matters of faith. We know we shall rise again. We are sure Christ will come again. But how this will happen will only be revealed to us when it occurs. Pictures help us to believe, but they should be seen as visible signs of invisible realities.

2. TRIBULATIONS

Millenarians argue that seven years of tribulations will accompany the last days. They base their position on the Last Judgment sermons of Jesus, the predictions of Daniel and Ezekiel, and the extensive lists of woes in the Apocalypse: the ones described by the seven seals, seven trumpets, and seven bowls of wrath.

But millenarians disagree as to when these will happen. One group says the tribulations will precede the thousand-year reign of Christ. The other school claims they will happen after the reign and just before the Second Coming.

So, the seven years of tribulations are either the second or third step of their four last things, depending on which school you follow. Since the battle of Armageddon is part of the age of tribulations there is a dispute as to when this occurs as well.

Catholic interpreters agree that tribulations will accompany the end of history just as Jesus and Apocalypse teach. Beyond that, little can be said. Virtually every century since Christ could claim to have had the very kinds of tribulations listed in the Apocalypse. If any century would be a champion, it is the twentieth. What period of history can surpass two world wars, the holocaust, Hiroshima and Nagasaki, the killing fields of Cambodia, the genocide of the Armenians, world hunger, the Depression, and many other woes?

Our century also had had its quota of famines, earthquakes, hurricanes — and some new threats such as global warming and tragedies related to lack of environmental concern. Yet the Second Coming has not occurred. Yes, there will be tribulations, but we do not know which are the ones that will actually signal the last days.

We should be less interested in tying these calamities to prophecies of the end time and expend more energy in probing the spiritual message of any tribulation. At the human level we use tragedies to learn lessons about life and how to improve conditions on earth. Do we not hope the twenty-first century will be a time of peace and prosperity and growth in faith after one hundred years of disasters? Blessed is the one who watches and prays, who is always personally prepared for the coming of the Lord, no matter when it will happen.

3. Millennium

The word millennium comes from two Latin words *mille* (meaning thousand) and *annus* (meaning year). Sometimes people speak of the millennium as *chiliasm*, from the Greek word *chilios* meaning "a thousand." Millenarians believe that the just are united with Jesus at the rapture and taken to heaven. Then there will be seven years of tribulations and the battle of Armageddon. Following this comes the thousand-year reign of Christ on earth. Jesus and the saints will rule the earth before the Second Coming. The kingdom of God will be realized on earth in a kind of Christian utopia.

The devil will lose his power at this time. John in Apocalypse says, "I also saw the souls of those who had been beheaded for their witness to Jesus. . . . They came to life and they reigned with Christ for a thousand years" (Rev 20:4). The rest of the dead will not rise until the end of the thousand years. The devil will be chained for this period but will be released at the conclusion of the millennium and cause the tribulations that precede the Second Coming. Then all people will be judged according to their deeds. Anyone whose name has not been written in the book of life will be thrown into the pool of fire (see Revelation 20:15).

Montanus Thought It Would Happen

This literal reading of the millennium occurred in the late second century Church under the leadership of a convert from paganism, Montanus of Asia Minor. Soon after his Baptism he gathered a group of followers who accepted his prediction that the heavenly Jerusalem would soon descend on the village of Pepuza. With the help of two disciples, Prisca and Maximilla, he preached intense asceticism, personal purity, and a burning desire for martyrdom.

His disciples accepted the idea that such a lifestyle was essential to prepare for the impending return of Christ. He advised husbands and wives to give up sexual relations and to live separately. His people spoke in tongues and attracted widespread attention. At his urging, people streamed into the countryside near Pepuza to await the millennium. Even though the New Jerusalem did not appear, the sect flourished and influenced many members of the Church. Its greatest convert was Tertullian in 207. The movement survived disappointments and the opposition of bishops until it died out in the sixth century.

Origen, a priest of Alexandria (185-254), broke the back of the literal reading of the millennium by giving it a symbolic meaning. Augustine completed what Origen had started. He said the thousand years meant the "era of the Church," the time between Christ's birth at Bethlehem and his Second Coming. The "rule of the saints," mentioned in the Apocalypse, is the victory of the kingdom of Christ in those human hearts that surrender to him in faith.

The judgment given to the saints is the power of the Sacrament of Reconciliation in which sins are bound and sinners released to freedom and forgiveness. The first resurrection described in Apocalypse chapter twenty is the welcoming into heaven of the saints who died before the Second Coming. Augustine gave a spiritual interpretation to this whole chapter and that is how the Catholic Church has accepted it ever since.

4. SECOND COMING

The final "last thing" of the millenarians is the Second Coming of Jesus and the last judgment. Christ will come to judge the living and the dead, send unrepentant sinners to hell, and welcome the just into heaven. I believe I have sufficiently noted that the millenarians continue to think they can nail down the date of this event despite repeated failures of earlier predictions. Each failure is followed by a reconsideration of some factor ignored in the previous prediction, thus allowing a new scenario to be proposed. It is a useless passion.

Catholics affirm their belief in the Second Coming with the words of the Nicene Creed, "He will come again in glory to judge the living and the dead." Though Catholics do not speak of the rapture, they do subscribe to the glorious, final manifestation of Jesus at the end of time.

Most discussions of the Second Coming concentrate so much on timing, or on the cosmic fireworks that will accompany it, that the spiritual value of the teaching is sometimes lost. Christ's promise to come again appeals to the millions of people whose lives are endangered by the daily troubles, trials, and tragedies to the point that hope is eroded. Life's indignities cause them to lose heart. The proverb says that hope springs eternal in the human heart, but in fact a great deal of hopelessness afflicts all too many people.

Many of them assume the best way to avoid this inner turmoil is to be convinced that Jesus is coming to end the present world and give them soon the promised happiness. Prophets of the imminent end time appeal to this yearning. "You can have hope if you know the millennium is at hand." I would view this as a spiritual escapism. St. Paul coped with the same problem with the Thessalonians. He learned how to tame their eagerness and train them to a spiritual discipline that equipped them for the long haul.

Their cry is, "Does God really care about us?" The Bible's answer is "yes." The Church's answer is "yes." Jesus has saved us. The Spirit is sanctifying us. The Father awaits our coming to the next life where he will glorify us. The Trinity provides this service for us in the Church and the Sacraments and the moral and spiritual guidance of the Magisterium.

The doctrine of the Second Coming of Jesus Christ is meant

to sustain the fire of our hope. No matter how terrible the ills we face in life, we can be certain that our Beloved will come to fulfill our deepest hopes. We might object that we will not be around for the actual Second Coming. We will most likely die before that great day. What good is a Second Coming we will probably never experience here? How can we keep moving through life's sea of troubles when we will probably not meet here the Beloved who says he is coming?

The answer is that Christ's Second Coming at the end of time has already begun. "Behold, I am with you always, even until the end of the world" (Mt 28:20). Human time does not restrict Jesus. A thousand years are like a second in his perspective. Jesus is already here, by the power of the Spirit.

What the final Second Coming will accomplish is a public display of his glory at the end of history. But we can already experience Christ's presence now. The Second Coming at the end of history will be a visible appearance of Jesus. His Second Coming today in our personal lives is an invisible one. St. Bernard tells us, "This coming is a hidden one. In it only the elect see the Lord within themselves." Jesus tells us that he comes to us right now as well as at the end of time.

Because we have, in faith, an immediate union with Jesus through the power of the Spirit, we have a guarantee of hope. This permits us to get on with our lives and releases the energies we need to love our neighbors, raise our families, work for peace and the elimination of poverty, cheer up the depressed, visit the sick, feed the homeless, and do many other acts of charity and mercy. The great religious drama need not be in the skies, but rather in a deeper place, the human heart. Every act of love for others enhances the growth of hope in our lives.

It is precisely at this point that I think the Church's four last things make the most sense.

THE CHURCH'S FOUR LAST THINGS

The Church's four last things are death, judgment, heaven, and hell. I offer you a brief reflection on each of these teachings.

Death

When two of the world's best-known women died in the same week, we were all reminded of our mortality. The paths of glory, whether for a young princess or for an elderly, saintly nun, lead to the grave. While death seems like an end to life, it is in reality a transition to another life. It is not the end of the world, but it is an end of "a" world and the beginning of another one. Christians unite their deaths to Christ and believe they are entering everlasting life. Life is changed, not taken away.

The Church wants to be present at the side of a dying Christian, sealing the believer with an anointing unto glory, pronouncing an absolution from sins, and giving Christ in the Eucharist as food for the final journey into the next life. At the funeral, the Church speaks with gentle assurance:

> Go forth, Christian soul, from this world . . .
> May you live in peace today.
> May your home be with God in Zion,
> with Mary, the virgin Mother of God,
> with Joseph, and all the angels and saints.
> Prayer of Commendation

For two thousand years Christians have died without witnessing the end of the world. They lived in a millennium that is the "era" of the Church. The only end they have known is the culmination of their lives on earth. They passed their years, saved by Christ, while struggling with the processes of sanctification offered to them by the Holy Spirit — more or less successfully. Many of them made extraordinary contributions to the well-being of the human race. Most of them offered smaller, less dramatic positive contributions, raising their families, doing their work, and bringing a modicum of cheer to their friends. Some, sadly, seem to have lived diminished lives, whose history we leave to God's judgment.

JUDGMENT

Before we die we have a life that is open to accepting or rejecting the grace of Christ. After death comes the divine judgment. The New Testament describes judgment in terms of Christ's Second Coming, but also states that each of us will be judged immediately after death. The parable of the poor man and Lazarus and Christ's words to the repentant thief on the cross reveal a final destiny which comes to us just after death and as the result of how we lived on earth.

Hence there is a particular judgment just after our deaths and a general judgment at the end of time. The soul survives death. The body will join the soul at the general resurrection of the dead. From one point of view we bring judgment upon ourselves by the way we have lived. From another aspect God is judging us, but his judgment simply confirms what we have already done with our lives.

We were given freedom to act lovingly, justly, and mercifully to all. God gave us the graces we needed to do this. We experienced these gifts of grace in the Church, the sacraments, the acts of love directed to us by others and the prayers of Mary and the saints. We were responsible for our lives on earth and must accept the consequences of our behavior. If we cooperated with grace we will go to heaven. If we did not, we face eternal damnation.

"At the evening of our life, we shall be judged only on our love" (St. John of the Cross, *Dichos*, 64).

HEAVEN

Those who die in friendship and grace with God, and who are perfectly purified, will live forever with Christ. They will see God face to face as he really is. This perfect life of love with the holy Trinity, with the Virgin Mary, the angels, and saints is called heaven. Heaven is the ultimate goal and realization of the deepest human desires. It is a state of supreme and ultimate happiness.

How great will your glory and happiness be,
to be allowed to see God, to be honored with
sharing the joy of salvation and eternal light
with Christ, your God . . . to delight in the joy
of immortality in the Kingdom of heaven with
the righteous and God's friends (St. Cyprian,
Letter 58, 10, 1).

PURGATORY

Some will die in God's grace and friendship, but are still imperfectly purified. We are assured of our eternal salvation, but after death we need further purification. We experience this purification in what the Church calls Purgatory. In the liturgy of All Souls on November 2, the Church remembers this teaching and recommends Eucharist, prayer, charitable giving, and works of penance on behalf of the departed. This teaching is based on the practice of prayer for the dead, already mentioned in the Bible. "Therefore, [Judas Maccabeus] made atonement for the dead, that they might be delivered from their sin" (2 Mac 12:46).

HELL

We cannot be united to God unless we freely choose to love him. We do not love God if we sin gravely against him, our neighbor, or ourselves. To die in mortal sin without repentance and recourse to God's mercy means we have separated ourselves from him by a deliberate and free choice. This definitive self-exclusion from communion with God is called hell.

Scripture and the teaching of the Church on heaven and hell emphasize a call to personal responsibility by which we use our freedom, aided by divine grace, to affect our eternal destiny. There is always an urgent call to conversion and repentance, especially during the seasons of Advent and Lent. God wants to save us, not to condemn us. Only a free turning away from God in mortal sin and persistence in this attitude leads to hell. The Church prays fervently every day for the conversion of sinners (see 2 Peter 3:9).

While we use earthly images, both physical and psychological, to describe heaven, hell, and purgatory, none of them comprehensively describes these mysterious realities. It is better for us to concentrate on sinless, loving choices, moral and spiritual responsibility, and lifelong conversion to Christ.

COMPARE THE TWO APPROACHES

When looking at the two versions of the four last things, it seems to me that the Catholic approach is the more realistic one. Despite eruptions of millenarian fever from time to time in Church history, among both Catholics and other Christians, most believers treat history as a matter of daily life, a time to love and serve and build up the family and society. They have worked on their salvation, with the help of God, with no need to anticipate some remarkable divine rescue operation that will end the slings and arrows of existence.

To their credit, however, we must admit that the millenarians do take seriously the doctrine of the Second Coming. Their fervent faith in this doctrine deserves our admiration. It lends energy to their spiritual lives and instills a courageous yearning for Christ. We Catholics can both admire and imitate that aspect of their religious attitudes.

On the other hand, the millenarians could learn from Catholics to approach the teaching as a mystery of faith that excludes dramatic dating of Christ's arrival and some of the extreme forms of behavior that this sometimes sustains. They might also adopt the Catholic view that, in a true sense, the Second Coming of Jesus has already begun, for Jesus has never abandoned us. Through the Spirit, Christ is living and active in the Church and in our lives. We should leave the final manifestation of his coming in public glory to the secret designs of the Father, just as Jesus advised his apostles so long ago.

Nevertheless, we can certainly join our millenarian friends in the prayer that occurs in the last verses of the Bible:

"Maranatha! Come, Lord Jesus" (Rev 22:20).

PART TWO

THE MILLENNIUM
AS A JUBILEE

FOR THE CHURCH, THE PEOPLE OF GOD, THE YEAR 2000 WILL BE THE YEAR OF A GREAT JUBILEE.
— POPE JOHN PAUL II
IN "MAN'S REDEEMER"

CHAPTER SEVEN:

CELEBRATE A JUBILEE

For Catholics, the third millennium is a Jubilee.

We praise God for his love and abundance of gifts. Christ has renewed his Church time and time again. For example:

In the fourteenth century the Church faced a crisis caused by the Avignon papacy. Popes had lived in Avignon, France, for nearly seventy years and had gradually become too involved with the French kings. These monarchs often used the papacy for political and economic gain. The result was widespread unhappiness in the universal Church, the cooling of faith, and the demoralizing of the clergy.

God raised up St. Catherine of Siena to be his instrument for renewing the Church. God called her to go to Avignon, where she would appeal to Pope Gregory XI to return to Rome. She rented a room across the Rhône River from the papal palace. She spent every day for four months meeting with the pope and employing numerous ways to convince him to leave. If she could not see him in person on a given day, she wrote him a letter.

From one point of view it is amazing that the pope permitted himself to be besieged by this formidable woman with no family connections, no formal education, no army, and none of the refinements of diplomacy. She had no illusions about the papal court, at which she said she smelled the "stench of sin."

She was disappointed in the weaknesses of Gregory. Unafraid, she said to him, "Be a man, Father! Arise! Don't be negligent. Begin the reform of the Church through appointing worthy priests. Make peace in Italy, not by force of arms, but by pardon and mercy. Return to Rome, not with swords and soldiers, but with the Cross and the blessed Lamb. O Father, peace, for the love of God" (Barbara Tuchman, *A Distant Mirror*).

Catherine was a loyal Catholic. She loved her Church. Her affection did not blind her to its shortcomings. One day she said to Gregory, "You are my sweet Jesus on earth." This was not empty flattery. She meant it. Sin and foolishness bothered her but they did not discourage her. She believed that where sin abounds, grace can abound even more. Human frailty is a challenge to call on the mighty river of God's healing love.

Her four-month campaign succeeded. Like the persistent widow of the Gospel who changed the mind of a judge (see Luke 18:1-5), she turned the heart of a pope and saw him off to Rome.

The Church honored Catherine by making her both a saint and a doctor of the Church. Today her statue stands on the Via della Conciliazione, the grand avenue that leads to the square of St. Peter's Basilica. Her head tilts toward the Vatican, her loving and prayerful eyes still alert, nudging the Church to constant renewal.

THE JUBILEE

Catherine's story is a cause for joy. She inspires us to thank God for the graces she received, and the gifts the Church obtained through her sanctity and courage. As the third millennium approaches, we have many reasons to celebrate God's gifts to the Church and the world awarded to us through the mediation of Jesus Christ.

Pope John Paul II has been thinking about the year 2000 since his election in 1978. In his first encyclical he wrote, "For the Church, the People of God, the year 2000 will be the year of a great Jubilee" ("Man's Redeemer," 1).

In 1994, the pope published an apostolic letter, *Tertio Adveniente Millennio*, "The Coming Third Millennium." In this letter he announced that the Church would treat the millennium as a year of Jubilee. He asked the Church to do the following things:

(1) Celebrate the 2,000th birthday of Jesus Christ. Our rejoicing encompasses Christ's entire messianic mission whereby he saved us from sin; planted God's Kingdom of love, justice, and mercy in our hearts; and gave us the Spirit, the Church, the Sacraments, and the Church's Teaching Office. Our Jubilee embraces all that Jesus means for the whole world, his mission from the Father, and his sending of the Spirit.

(2) The millennium should also be a time of repentance for the sins done in the name of the Church as well as an occasion for each of us to repent of our sins.

(3) This event should motivate us to take up with renewed energy the call for all Christians to be reconciled and united into one Christianity. This means the ecumenical movement should be renewed with greater love and prayer, so that all Christian churches may be one in Christ.

(4) The year 2000 should awaken the enthusiasm of the Church for a new evangelization of nations. Jesus Christ came to us out of love to save every human being from sin and invite everyone into God's family of divine life and eternal friendship with God. With prayer, love, and affection, we should share our faith with all people who have not yet received this wondrous gift.

(5) A Jubilee is a perfect time to renew the Church's commitment to justice, freedom, peace, and a fulfilling life for every person on earth. The seeds of the Church's social teachings are found in the biblical account of creation and the attempt to implement the meaning of creation in Old Testament Jubilee years.

(6) There should be a Trinitarian preparation for the Jubilee:

> 1997 — The Year of Christ
> 1998 — The Year of the Spirit
> 1999 — The Year of the Father

I will provide a reflection for each of these years in the next chapters.

THE JUBILEE IN SCRIPTURE

The custom of Jubilees began in the Old Testament and continues in the history of the Church. A biblical Jubilee was a time dedicated to God. One version of it fell every seventh year. During this sabbatical year the earth was left fallow and slaves were set free. The Book of Exodus (23:10-11) and other books laid down the rules for liberating the slaves. The rules also called for canceling debts. People were expected to follow these laws to increase the honor of God.

Every fifty years biblical people also celebrated a Jubilee year. The customs of the sabbatical year were expanded and given greater solemnity. Every Israelite should regain his ancestral land if it happened to have been sold or lost because of falling into slavery. Ever since God had liberated Israel from slavery in Egypt, it became an ideal that no Israelite should be without land or remain a slave.

The Jubilee created an expectation that all the children of Israel would be equal. It offered new possibilities to families who had lost their land and even their freedom. It reminded the rich that a day would come when Israelite slaves would reclaim their rights and become their equals.

Unhappily, the rules for a Jubilee year remained more an ideal than an actual fact. But these dreams did become a prophecy of the future when the Messiah would win peoples' freedom. We might well see in these teachings the seeds of a social doctrine that would take many centuries to nourish and bring to flower.

The religious teaching embedded in the Jubilee year was based on the people's faith that God is the Lord of creation. God created the land and its natural resources. It belongs to the owner, the Creator. But God is also a Provider, a Provident God. God gave the earth to people.

Hence the riches of creation are meant for the common

good of all people to help them raise a family, provide for the future , and live a fulfilling human life. People, therefore, are but stewards of God's creation. The steward should implement the will of the owner. It is God's will that created good should serve everyone in a just manner. This vision of social justice achieved a special development in the Church's social doctrine after the industrial revolution and has evolved in the twentieth century in response to numerous global problems and the arrival of the technological revolution.

THE YEAR OF THE LORD'S FAVOR

Recall again the story of Jesus going to his hometown Nazareth to preach his first sermon in the synagogue (read Luke 4:14-30). Visualize the scene. The synagogue was a simple, unadorned room designed for prayer and religious instruction. People sat around a small platform on which there was a chair and a reading stand. The service consisted of an opening prayer, a reading from the Bible, a sermon, and a closing discussion.

Jesus had already acquired a modest fame from his preaching and miracles in other communities. Now he was on home territory. Everyone knew Jesus as a respected carpenter among them for many years. They honored his widowed mother. Admiring news about him had drifted in from all over Galilee. They anticipated a satisfying prayer meeting led by one of their own.

After the opening prayer, the administrator gave Jesus a scroll on which was written Chapter sixty-one of Isaiah. Jesus read the text in Hebrew and then translated the text into Aramaic, for most listeners no longer understood ancient Hebrew.

He closed the scroll, gave it back to the presiding officer and sat down to comment on the text. The verses he read spoke of the Spirit anointing the Messiah for the purpose of preaching the Good News to the poor. This was a preaching to be matched by good works: liberating prisoners, freeing the oppressed, and healing the blind. The Messiah would ". . . proclaim a year acceptable to the Lord" (Lk 4:19). In other words, a Jubilee.

These words gripped the hearts of the listeners. They knew all about the tradition of the Jubilee. They ached for the fulfillment of the prophecy Jesus read in a time when their experience was one of oppression from the Roman rulers. They had relatives and friends who languished in prisons for defying the army of occupation. They felt the humiliating sting of not being masters in their own homes. The impulse to revolution was close to the surface.

Jesus knew the explosive political context that gave urgency to the words of Isaiah. But he came to give an interpretation of the prophet which dealt with salvation from sin and the arrival of the Kingdom of God — an experience that calls for the graced conversion of every human heart. Redemption from sin and its effects would bring about God's rule of love, justice, mercy, and service in the human heart, from which it would flow into practical application in the social order. That is the Jubilee Christ preached.

He had paused and let the silence focus everyone's attention.

Then ". . . Today this scripture passage is fulfilled in your hearing" (Lk 4:21). Jesus says he is the Messiah Isaiah foretold.

His listeners were not ready to accept a hometown boy as Messiah and they certainly did not want a spiritual interpretation of the passage. They became so angry they wanted to kill him. Jesus miraculously walked away from their murderous arms and his village.

Nonetheless, the fullness of time had come in Jesus Christ. The day of salvation had come in Christ. His "time" was the greatest and most authentic of all Jubilees. Every Jubilee the Church would subsequently celebrate points back to the time of Christ and to his messianic mission — sent by the Father and anointed by the Spirit to save and sanctify the world. Jesus would establish the spiritual possibilities that would make the moral and social renewal of the world a realizable fact.

When contrasted to the views of the millennium as the end of the world as outlined in the first half of this book, Pope John Paul's vision is quite different. For him the year 2000 is a beginning of a new advent of Christ for the world. He does not allude to chapter twenty of Revelation or to any apocalyptic type of interpretation of the coming millennium. Of course, like all of us, the pope believes in and teaches the Second Coming of Christ and the final manifestation of the Lord's glory and the Last Judgment. But that is a different question than the issue of the forthcoming celebration of the third millennium.

HOW SHOULD WE PREPARE FOR THE THIRD MILLENNIUM?

We should praise God for the gifts of the Incarnation, the Church, the sacraments. the holiness of the saints, the forgiveness of sins, and the joy of conversions. The abundance of divine graces meant to enrich our humanity and bring us to eternal life ought to penetrate our hearts with gratitude to our all-loving God. Our faith is based upon a religion of abundance, not a theology of scarcity. The Holy Eucharist contains the entire wealth of the Church, Jesus Christ himself. This Eucharist is both our song of thanksgiving as well as our Bread for the journey to the kingdom.

The pope says, "Open wide the doors!" He is thinking of the custom of opening the Holy Door of St. Peter's during Holy Years. That lovely custom is more than a ceremonial gesture. It is an act that symbolizes what we need to do with the doors of our hearts as well as what the universal Church needs to do.

Since the last millennium in the year 1000, the Church has suffered the wound of disunity. First was the Eastern Schism and then came the Protestant Reformation. We need now to open the doors of love and a prayerful heart that the Spirit will endow us with a new Pentecost of ecclesial unity. Naturally, we should do all we humanly can to facilitate the union of all the Christian churches. But we will need the graces of the Spirit to bring about the desired unity of the Christian churches.

The Jubilee should be a time for personal spiritual renewal. This involves repentance for our sins and a fresh moral conversion. The Sacrament of Reconciliation is available to us for this purpose. We should plan to make the best confession of our whole lives. Conversion also includes engaging ourselves in the renewal of our spiritual lives. This means a revival of our prayer life, our commitment to meditation, and the deepening of our desire for God.

In laying aside our vices, we are challenged to acquire the virtues that will crowd out the sinful sides of our lives. The word *virtue* comes from a Latin word that means "force and power." Resistance to vice is easier when we have learned to practice the good habits that orient us to God. Virtues groove the moral order into our souls. Virtues empower us to act morally. We gain the life of virtue by being inspired by the lives of the saints and other inspiring people. It also helps to notice the good example of people around us. A virtue support group makes the task easier.

Next, virtue is acquired by practice. Repetition of virtuous acts is the secret of growing in the desired virtue. Finally, constant prayer to the Holy Spirit will obtain for us the graces we need for the life of virtue. Every day, talk over your life with the Holy Spirit, reviewing yesterday's wins and losses. Keep asking the Spirit for the virtue you want.

THE LIFE OF FAITH

It is obvious now that Jubilee 2000 should be a time of Christian action whereby we grow in gratitude for salvation, strive for the unity of all Christians, repent of our sins, and make a fresh commitment to the life of virtue. By our Baptisms we were made "new beings" in Christ. The outcome for a new being is spiritual renewal inwardly and acts of love, justice, mercy, and service outwardly.

All this will require a faith perspective that will penetrate our awareness and influence our deeds. Faith is the driving force of our Catholic life. In faith we meet Jesus Christ and become his friend, accepting the salvation he offers us and agreeing to the conditions of a saved life.

Faith is a personal act, an I/thou relationship with Jesus. It is also a community act. Every Sunday in the Nicene Creed, the first words said are, "We believe." Catholicism is more than an individualistic religion. We cannot be Lone Rangers of the spirit, riding the trails of life by ourselves. Faith tells us that we work together for the coming of the kingdom, supporting one another in thought, word, and deed. It is easier for me to believe in Jesus if I know that others around me have the same belief. The power of the community of worship and faith reinforces my ability to believe.

Our faith is always a gift of divine grace from the Holy Spirit. That is why we say of converts that they have received the "gift of faith." Some people speak of faith as a "leap of faith." In one sense this might be true, but in another sense it fails to communicate the giftedness of faith. A leap makes it sound as if we are doing it. It situates the act in our own efforts. Certainly the acts we perform can open us to the gift of faith such as nurturing our search for truth and for God and sustaining an open heart. Still, we await the grace that comes from God alone.

Some years ago the Jewish philosopher and Great Books advocate Mortimer Adler was very popular in Catholic circles because of his lucid presentations of the teachings of Thomas Aquinas. He had a reputation for knowing St. Thomas as well as or even better than many Catholic scholars. Frequently, he heard the question, "Why haven't you become a Catholic?" His favorite answer, "Because I take seriously the teaching of Aquinas. Faith is a gift. I have not received this gift."

Faith also embraces the knowledge and acceptance of the truths and doctrines of the Church. There is a line in an old song: "Getting to know you, getting to know all about you."

These lines capture the two poles of faith, one being the relationship between us and Jesus (getting to know you), and the meaning of that relationship (getting to know all about you).

If I love someone, will I not want to know the truth about the beloved?

This is why the *Catechism of the Catholic Church* is such a treasure for true believers. It is a book of truths about our beloved Jesus Christ. When we love Christ, we will want to know all we can about him. One of the special advantages of the *Catechism* is its clear use of the Bible, integrating Scripture into the doctrinal content. There are three thousand Scripture references in the *Catechism*.

It should be one of the goals of a Catholic to be religiously literate, able to know the major truths of the faith and to be able to explain and defend them. Whenever we seek to share our faith with others, we will feel more confident if we have an intelligent and coherent grasp of Church teachings. Such mastery also helps achieve Catholic identity. Religious knowledge contributes to answering the question, Who is a Catholic?

Still we should never forget that knowing the facts of faith is only part of a grand tapestry of the dimensions of faith. We must not forget that faith is a love relationship with Christ, a gift from the Holy Spirit, a communal as well as an individual act. When we appreciate these broad and essential aspects of faith, we will have the assurance and conviction to which we aspire.

It is always a joy to read the Book of Hebrews, chapter eleven. The author devotes the whole chapter to a praise of faith as it has appeared in the lives of biblical figures. Examples of faith abound all the way from Abraham to Mary and beyond. The first verse, however, should capture our attention.

> Faith is the assurance of things hoped for,
> the conviction of things not seen (RSV Heb 11:1).

Convinced people convince others. People expect Catholics to have conviction and assurance about their religion. This is not always easy for cradle Catholics who become accustomed to their religion and are not inclined to probe its depths both in terms of a vital relationship with Jesus and a holy curiosity about its teachings. These Catholics acquire spiritual cataracts, the film of familiarity that breeds indifference to the adventure and excitement inherent in their religion.

Contrast this with the fervor that converts bring to Catholicism. Three of the greatest theologians in Church history were converts: Paul, Augustine, and Cardinal Newman. They brought to the Church their brilliant minds and burning hearts. Their influence on the faith of the Church is so extraordinary that there is no measure to encompass it. They remind us that conviction and assurance in our faith attitudes are both possible and necessary.

Other obvious examples of conviction and assurance are the lives of the saints, whether they be contemplatives in cloisters like Thérèse of Lisieux or adventurous activists like the missionary Francis Xavier and the apostle to the poor —Vincent de Paul. It took a lot of conviction to bolster the courage of Thomas More when faced with the power of the English crown. It demanded an enormous amount of assurance for the nineteen-year-old Joan of Arc to stand up to one hundred bishops at her "heresy" trial and hold her own. Only a truly faith-filled young woman could answer this question so aptly:

Bishops: "Joan, are you in the state of grace?"
Joan: "If I am, may God keep me there.
            "If I am not, may God put me there."

The Jubilee 2000 should be an occasion of profound spiritual renewal for the Catholic Church. Once again we should tune up the ears of our hearts to hear the call to holiness that comes to us from our heavenly Father. We need to be prepared to recommit ourselves to Jesus Christ, who loved us even to death, in such a way that our Baptisms and Confirmations are made alive once more in our lives. We ought to let the Holy Spirit dwell in our bodies as in a Temple.

Only fervent prayer, worship, and faith can make this happen.

Pope John Paul II frequently turns our attention to our Blessed Mother Mary, inviting us to appeal to her intercession to help us embrace in a fresh way our journey of faith. Mary's last words in Scripture were, "Do whatever he tells you" (Jn 2:5). At Cana Mary fulfilled two of her duties, one to intercede with Jesus on behalf of the embarrassed couple and second to remind you and me that we should always be prepared to do what Jesus asks of us.

At Calvary, just before he died, Jesus spoke to Mary and asked her to look after the "son," meaning the sons and daughters who would be born in the church through Baptism. Pope Paul VI probed this mysterious saying and came to the conclusion that he could call Mary the Mother of the Church. More than anyone else, Mary will be celebrating Jubilee 2000, both for the joy it will bring to Jesus and for the renewal it makes possible for the Catholic Church.

No, the third millennium is not the end of the world.

Yes, the third millennium is the beginning of a new time of hope for the Church.

John Paul has set this tone of expectation for us, and we should bring hope to the world by allowing the beauty of the Church to be available to the millions who need Christ.

It's "party time" in the best sense of the words.

CHAPTER EIGHT:

O JESUS, JOY OF LOVING HEARTS

O Jesus, ever with me stay.
Make all my moments calm and bright.
O chase the night of sin away.
Shed o'er the world your holy light.

HE'S OURS AND WE LOVE HIM

In 1945 a baby was born to Mary Teresa Hickey and her husband, Dan. The parents came from Cork, Ireland.

The baby was a Down's Syndrome boy.

Mary Teresa held the baby tightly, saying, "He's ours and we love him. He is God's chosen one."

The family lived on Train Street in the Dorchester section of Boston. Their other boy was Jimmy. The dad died young of a heart attack, and Mary was left to raise the two boys, nine-year-old Jimmy and seven-year-old Danny. To pay the rent she scrubbed floors at the old Chronic Care Hospital in Mattapan.

Jimmy took good care of Danny. Dan felt at home with all the kids because no one told him he was different. Then one day they were boarding a trackless trolley at Fields Corner and some strange kids shouted, "No morons on the bus!" That was the day Jimmy Hickey learned to fight. It was also the day Jimmy decided to be a priest. Little Danny attended the Kennedy school in Brighton and eventually obtained a job at Work, Inc.

In 1991, Mary Teresa Hickey died at age ninety-one after showering her sons with unyielding love all their lives.

Father Jim Hickey has been a priest for thirty years. In

every parish to which he was assigned, Danny went along with him. The people were favored with both men.

In October 1997, Danny was in Bringham and Women's Hospital. His fifty-two-year-old body was failing. One night when ordinary people were eating supper, watching a ballgame or going to a movie, a simple story of brotherly love played itself out at the bedside of a man who never felt sorry for himself or thought he was different.

Father Jim held his brother and asked, "Do you trust me, Danny?"

"I trust you."

"You're going to be OK."

"I be OK."

Eight hundred people stood in line at his wake.

Parishioners packed Holy Family Church for his funeral.

They sang and cried and prayed.

Later that day, Daniel Jeremiah Hickey was gently laid beside his parents at New Calvary cemetery.

The granite headstone bore his name and the inscription:

"God's Chosen"

(Adapted from a column by Mike Barnicle, *Boston Globe*.)

JESUS LOVES ME

The inspiring story of the Hickey family shows what happens when Christ's saving love warms the hearts of parents and their children. Pope John Paul II's vision of the millenium invites us to experience again the remarkable love of Jesus Christ — a love that saved us from our sins and guilt and lights a fire of affection within our hearts.

Let the year 2000 be a joyful "yes" to Jesus our Savior who is both the Son of God and the Son of Mary. Our preparation for the millennium deserves a continued appreciation of Christ's work as our Savior and Christ's identity as the God-man. I will take each of these themes in turn.

JESUS OUR SAVIOR

We should begin with three key verses from John's Gospel.

> For God so loved the world that he gave his only Son, so that everyone who believes in him might not perish but might have eternal life (Jn 3:16).

> For God did not send his Son into the world to condemn the world, but that the world might be saved through him (Jn 3:17).

> And when he [the Spirit] comes he will convict the world in regard to sin. . . (Jn 16:8).

Now look at the first two tremendous verses, John 3:16-17. They speak of God's motivation — love for the world. And his purpose in loving us — our salvation from sin. Just as important, notice that Jesus did not come to condemn us, but to save us. This reminds me of Christ's touching words to the woman taken in adultery, "Neither do I condemn you. Go and sin no more" (see John 8:11).

Jesus doesn't approach us with a condemning attitude. He has not gone to all the trouble to take on our humanity and live within our world to scold us. Jesus has boundless compassion for our weaknesses. He made the incredible effort to see what it is like to be human so he could comfort and save us, not reproach us. Jesus is no angry God waiting to catch us in our sins. Jesus is a merciful Savior trying to rescue us from our guilt. Jesus is our shepherd, not a mean-spirited tyrant.

John's verses use the term "world" twice.

Does this word "world" have any relevance for us?

In general, the world is another name for the *culture* in which people find themselves. The apostles and missionaries of the early Church were able to convert much of the known world because the culture recognized God's presence and human sinfulness. Those ancient peoples believed not only in the existence of God, but also in the reality of sin.

True, many of the pagans had a confused idea of God, sometimes identifying God with the sun or moon or stars or even with the emperor. But they would have thought it strange for someone to ask, "Does God exist? Or, does a God exist?" And while they may have had a weak moral sense in some cases, they generally admitted the existence of sin, guilt, and moral issues. Our first evangelizers encountered a culture that knew of God and sin. What they needed was the truth about God's plan to love us and save us from our sins in the crucified and risen Jesus Christ. The powerful message of the Gospel converted a world.

BUT WHAT ABOUT THE "WORLD" TODAY?

Today the world or the culture thinks differently because of a change in the history of human thought that began with Decartes three centuries ago. He was a good Christian attempting to solve some philosophical problems caused by his interest in mathematical theory. He became famous for his dictum, "I think, therefore, I am."

He moved western culture: From *what* we think about — the evidence of the senses and things — to *who* is doing the thinking — the processes of our minds.

My mind becomes the focus of my energies, not the external world that feeds the mind with pictures, images, stories, impressions, facts, data, etc. What happened as a result of this? Well, the more people retreated into their inner world, the less the outer world seemed real or important.

Subsequent philosophers began to say, "Reality does not shape my thought. My thought shapes reality. My inner world is far more exciting and true than the concrete, physical existence outside me. If it exists in my thinking, it is true. If it isn't in my mind, it does not exist elsewhere. Objective reality doesn't matter. Subjective reality does."

Subjective reality became triumphant: *I think.*

The next phase was taken up by the eighteenth-century Enlightenment. First, God was pushed beyond this world to some margin. God is simply a clockmaker. He made the clock. It's up to us to take care of it, wind it up, and manage it. Knowledge of God became useless. We should live by reason alone.

It should be noted here that Decartes did not plan for all this to happen. He was good Christian wrestling with philosophical problems of his time. His theories became the victim of the "law of unintended consequences."

Time marched on, however. The world or the culture today tells us, "I do not need God. I do not need divine love. I do not need salvation from my sins — I have no sin." This radical aspect of modern culture claims that science can solve all mysteries. Technology has plenty of raw materials to make this happen. It's only a matter of time. Let's face it, only the world can make us happy because it gives us:

a workshop that creates knowledge;

a communications wonderland; and

the growing list of democratic societies without limits.

In all fairness I need to say that not all thoughtful scientists, philosophers, or arbiters of contemporary culture buy this vision. There are thousands, perhaps millions, of people of goodwill who are struggling with the culture, attempting to establish a wholesome moral order and restore a vision of a concerned God for the modern world.

The celebration of the millennium gives us a chance to proclaim again that Jesus loves the world and wants to save it, not condemn it. When Jesus used the term "world" in John 3:16-17, he was thinking of the first chapter of the Book of Genesis. In that story of creation, God smiles on all he created and said, "That's good!" As many have said, "God does not make junk." God loved a good creation into existence.

But this good world — whether it be the favorable culture of New Testament times or the unfavorable culture of our own day — does not assure salvation. The world cannot make us happy. It is not able to save us completely from all physical evils. We thank God for the amazing advances in medicine, but we still get the common cold. There will always be need for doctors.

The world is not able to liberate us from death. Immortality is a gift from God, not from the world. Neither the pyramids of Egypt nor the cryonic freezers of Hollywood are assurances of immortality. They are interesting efforts to make it happen and are actually fascinating symbols of our hunger to last forever.

Third, the world cannot save us from sin. A culture that denies sin will hardly try to save us from it. As an heir of the Enlightenment, modern culture seems bent on denying both original and actual sin. But denial does not get rid of what is denied. Like it or not, sin exists.

AWARENESS OF SIN

Jesus knew that we need help to recognize our sinfulness. At the Last Supper Jesus promised the apostles that he would send them the Holy Spirit. One of the duties of the Spirit would be to make us aware of our sinfulness, not to depress us with guilt but to help us know our sins and so be able to be saved from them by the forgiving power of Christ through the Sacrament of Reconciliation.

John 16:8 says the Spirit will come to *convict* us of sin. Jesus described the Spirit as a "Paraclete," a sort of lawyer. This divine lawyer would take us through a three-step process. The Spirit's first task is to *convince* us of our sinfulness. Secondly, to *convict* us. Finally, to *convert* us from our sinfulness. So, we should not give a narrow interpretation to the expression "convict" in John 16:8.

Convincing the world of sin is not the same as condemning the world. Convincing means creating the conditions for the world's salvation. This process involves the followings stages:

Become aware of the reality of sin;

Acknowledge that Jesus is our Savior who wants to love away our sin and guilt; and

Open our hearts to Christ in the Sacrament of Reconciliation.

Think of the mercy of the Father to the Prodigal Son and the kindness of Jesus to the woman taken in adultery. He did not condemn her. He saved her and told her not to sin again.

As a result of this we are convinced of our sins, convicted of them, converted from them. Jesus our Savior lifts us up with redemptive love. Christ's love is always greater than any sin we can commit.

JESUS — GOD AND MAN

Jesus is able to save us from our sins and give us both immortality and eternal life, an experience we have already here in earth because of divine grace. Jesus could do this because he is the Son of God incarnate in a human nature. Jesus is radically different from other great figures of world religions.

Jesus is not just a Mohammed. Jesus did more than communicate principles of religious discipline. Jesus is more than a religious disciplinarian. Jesus is our Savior.

Jesus is not just a wise philosopher like Socrates. Jesus was certainly a wise leader. The Gospels are full of his wisdom sayings, such as those in the Sermon on the Mount. But Jesus is more than a teacher. Jesus is our Savior.

Jesus is not just like Buddha who taught the value of meditation and a suspicion of creation. Jesus taught his apostles to pray, and he spent whole nights in contemplation in the mountains. Jesus did not have a suspicion of creation. As the Word of God, creation was created through him. Jesus eternally witnessed his Father creating the universe and speaking of the goodness of creation, especially the creation of man and woman . . . male and female in the image and likeness of God. Jesus is more than a meditation mentor. Jesus is our Savior.

Jesus is totally original and unique.

Jesus is really human. Vatican II puts it this way: "The Son of God . . . worked with human hands; he thought with a human mind. He acted with a human will, and with a human heart he loved. Born of the Virgin Mary, he has truly been made one of us, like to us in all things except sin" ("Church in the Modern World," 22).

No other human is also divine. Read:

Matthew 16:16 — "You are the Messiah, the Son of the living God."

Luke 10:22 — "No one knows who the Son is except the Father, and who the Father is except the Son. . . ."

John 1:1,14 (The Hymn to the Word Incarnate) — "In the beginning was the Word, and the Word was with God and the Word was God. And the Word became flesh. . . ."

Philippians 2:11 — ". . . Jesus Christ is Lord" (the expression "Lord" here is *Kyrios* in Greek and means God).

The New Testament clearly asserts the divinity of Jesus Christ as well as his humanity. All the Ecumenical Councils of the Church in the first millennium, the first one thousand years of Christianity, clarified the meaning of Jesus as truly God and Man. The Council Fathers said that Jesus had a divine nature and a human nature — united by a divine Person. *Not a human person, but a divine one.*

Because of the divine person, the human acts of Jesus could save us from our sins and give us divine life through the ministry of the Church and her sacraments. Christ is explosive! Theologians and saints never get enough of exploring Jesus in the New Testament and his prefiguring in the Old Testament.

GET READY TO SHARE THE GOOD NEWS

This great news about Jesus Christ should be shared joyfully with the world in the coming third millennium.

> Go, therefore, and make disciples of all nations, baptizing them in the name of the Father, and of the Son, and of the holy Spirit, teaching them to observe all that I have commanded you. . . (Mt 28:19-20).

Pope John Paul II, who walks in the shoes of the fisherman, is an outstanding example of one who has heard Christ's call to share the Good News of salvation. He has traveled to more than eighty countries to conduct what he calls the "Dialogue of Salvation."

In August 1997, he went to Paris for World Youth Day. The French bishops worried that the crowd would not be very big — only 300,000! — because the weather would be too hot and because France is only nominally a Catholic country. Barely 10 percent of the people go to Mass on Sunday. Were they pleasantly surprised!

On Friday of the pope's visit, 500,000 young people crowded around him at the Eiffel Tower. On Saturday night, 800,000 gathered with him for Baptisms, after which they sang and danced. On Sunday for the Mass at Longchamps, 1,200,000 assembled for the glorious climax of an astonishing weekend of faith and worship around the man who wears the shoes of the fisherman. It was the largest assembly in Paris in one place in history and in 95-degree heat.

Paris said it would be bored by an old man with outdated moral teachings. The "fisherman" is irrelevant. Yet 45 percent of France watched the pope's Mass on TV. Commentators talked about the visit for days afterwards. They recalled that it used to be said that the Beatles were more popular than Jesus. The Beatles never drew a crowd like the pope's.

Many young people were interviewed and said they were skeptical about the pope's views on birth control, abortion, and women's ordination. "Then, why are you here?" "Because of the pope, the fisherman."

How do you resolve this contradiction? The youth admire John Paul's faith and courage. Many of them are from Generation X — the children of the baby boomers, the '60s parents. The anthem of that period distilled its spirit:

> When the moon is in the seventh house,
> and Jupiter aligns with Mars,

Then peace will guide the planets,
And love will steer the stars.
This is the dawning of the Age of Aquarius.

Today's youth argue that astrology isn't enough. Many of their parents had said, "No more hierarchy, patriarchy, moral code." This did not work. A number of young people felt deserted without moral standards and some respect for tradition. They are the children of confusion.

They are attracted to an old man who really does believe in God, divine revelation, self-sacrifice, and objective morality. They cry for faith. A *cri de coeur*. "We must look elsewhere . . . to the man who wears the shoes of the fisherman." The papers showed a picture of a sign that said to the pope, "You are our youth."

The pope is an evangelist just like St. Peter was. He roams the world sharing the joy of his faith in Jesus. He asks his listeners to cross the threshold of hope. He is firm about the doctrines and moral teachings of the Church. But he always speaks the truth in love. He tries to stir up hope in a culture that often has lost its moral compass.

Pope John Paul has frequently said he wants the third millennium to be the age of the new evangelization. He practices what he preaches and shows us how to get out of our narrow confines and be willing to share our faith with others.

I had the good fortune to know another fine evangelizer, the Paulist Father Alvin Illig. Single handedly he put evangelization on the agenda of the Church in the United States. He established an office for evangelization at the Paulist College in Washington, D.C.

Alvin was proud of the fact that he was in the first group of seminarians to be ordained by Bishop Fulton Sheen, himself a marvelous evangelizer. Alvin sensed that a love of Scripture was the best way to generate an evangelizing spirit. This led him to enlist talent to create "Share the Word," which linked Scripture study and prayer to the Sunday liturgies.

Father Illig was a practical man who knew how to take religion out of the scholar's tower and bring it to the parish church and the public square. Fascinated by the possibilities of the new media, he pioneered national evangelization meetings using satellite technology. He also sponsored the making of videocassette programs on Scripture. For him, the communications revolution was a gift from God to share the message of Christ. As he often said, "I take the electronic word to proclaim the divine Word."

This great Paulist priest lived by the dictum "I don't want to be so heavenly minded that I'm no earthly good." His clear vision served his deep faith. "Will the goal in faith and you will find the legitimate means to achieve it." He never believed in panaceas. He was not committed to one, single way to evangelize. Let there be a variety of methods adapted to the wide range of people we will meet. Like his beloved St. Paul, the patron of his congregation, he raced along with his culture to give the world the prize of Christ's salvation.

In the third millennium God calls us to renew our faith in Jesus our Savior and deepen our understanding of the mystery of the Son of God made man. Our Father invites us to share our faith with others, to become a partner in the new evangelization.

We need to awaken our minds and hearts to the beauty of the divine love that came to save us from sin and fill us with divine life. Jesus did not come to condemn us, but to love us and save us. This will require an awareness of our sinfulness. The Holy Spirit is here to convince us of our sinfulness, convict us, and then convert us from all that is evil.

The Good News of salvation should prompt us to go forth and share our faith with others. The culture seems hostile on the one hand because it has lost the sense of God's presence in the world and denies the reality of sin. But on the other hand, the hunger for God has never disappeared, nor has the inner need for wholeness, another way of speaking about the desire for forgiveness for sins. People do want to be liberated from evil, but they are sheep without a shepherd. They are lost.

God has been very good to us. God has loved us into grace. We can be the shepherds the world desires. Look at the example of Pope John Paul II, now an old man, stooped over, trembling with Parkinson's disease, yet he is a magnet for millions of young people and countless others.

Convinced people convince others.

It's our turn now.

CHAPTER NINE:

SANCTIFIED BY THE SPIRIT

Breathe on me, Breath of God,
My soul with grace refine,
Until this earthly part of me,
Glows with your fire divine.

The last time we had a pope who was not an Italian (prior to John Paul II) was in 1522. His name was Adrian VI, and he was a Dutchman. There is a story told that he commissioned a painting of the biblical scene "The Storm at Sea," based on Matthew 14:22-33. The artist decided to call the picture "The Ship of Peter," since it was Peter's boat that encountered the tempest.

The day came for the unveiling of the work. In the picture the pope saw a handsome ship — like a Spanish galleon — floating on a still sea of glass. The sails hung quietly from the mast. On the deck, the pope knelt in prayer surrounded by a devout cluster of cardinals. Below, in the staterooms, the Catholics peered out through the square portholes.

Beyond this serene tableau, at the edges of the painting, were storms, waves, and fierce winds. Flailing desperately in these tumultuous waters were the Protestants, Jews, and Muslims, separated from the ship of Peter by the silent sea and the protected people on board.

Pope Adrian stared at the picture and then erupted in anger. "No, this is all wrong. This is not what the text of Matthew tells us. Peter and the apostles are in the midst of the storm. The scene should also reflect the historical fact that the Church, from the beginning, has faced a succession of storms." The pope recalled to the artist the words of Psalm 107, which so vividly described a sea storm, the prayer of the sailors, and the rescue from God.

> They mounted up to heaven;
>> they sank to the depths;
>> their hearts melted away in their plight.
> They reeled and staggered like drunken men . . .
> They cried to the LORD in their distress;
>> from their straits he rescued them.
> He hushed the storm to a gentle breeze . . .
>> (Ps 107: 26-29).

This painting gave no indication that the pope, the cardinals, and the Catholics were part of a real world or would be involved in life's storms. It was an unreal scene that robbed the Church of any concern for those who were in the tumults of life. Adrian pressed his ring against the canvas at either end. "We must be saved with these and these and these!" After all, was it not Peter himself who cried out in the story, "Lord, save me!"

THE SPIRIT IS THE DYNAMISM OF GOD

This story reminds us that the Church has been sailing stormy seas for two thousand years. It also tells us that the Church continues to experience God's saving power no matter how great the tempest.

Jubilee 2000 is an occasion for celebrating this abiding, loving concern for the Church by the Spirit of God. Not just for the Church, but for the world itself.

We praise the Holy Spirit for the ongoing gift of sanctification.

How should we celebrate the Holy Spirit in the forthcoming third millennium? I suggest the following three ways to do this:

(1) Share with others a catechesis of the Holy Spirit.

(2) Renew your Confirmation commitment.

(3) Make visible the Love of the Spirit in our world.

To assist you in this calling, I offer you reflections on each of these elements.

SHARE WITH OTHERS A CATECHESIS OF THE SPIRIT

Who is the Holy Spirit?

Theologically, the Spirit is the third person of the Holy Trinity. The Spirit is the equal of the Father and the Son. With them the Spirit should be worshipped and glorified. The Spirit is the Lord and giver of life. We pray these truths every Sunday in the Nicene Creed.

Experientially, the Spirit provides us with a sense of the presence of God. When we have known the dynamic impact of God on our lives, we have the Spirit to thank for that. Sometimes this happens with a palpable feeling of God's presence with its accompanying joy. Just as often there are no religious feelings, but a quieter, religious conviction, even in the midst of intractable problems and sufferings. Amazingly we still believe. The New Testament frequently associates the Greek word *dynamis* (dynamism) with the influence of the Spirit.

Permit me to use a biblical catechesis of the Spirit because the scriptural symbols and pictures help us to grasp the invisible powers of the Spirit working in our hearts. I share with you these five "pictures" of the Spirit.

FIVE BIBLICAL "PICTURES" OF THE SPIRIT

I. BREATH

Genesis begins with the scene of a dark and stormy sea, the chaos. Scripture says that God "breathed" over the void and began the process of creation. The Hebrew word for breath is *Ruah*.

The breath of God is the first hint about the Holy Spirit, whose creative action brings order out of the mess of the universe. God's breath brings the chaos to an orderly cosmos.

Compare this scene with the Upper Room on Easter night. In John's Gospel, the newly risen Christ appeared to the fearful and chaotic apostles after sundown on Easter. He breathed on them and said, "Receive the holy Spirit." (Jn 20:22) The Spirit transformed the disoriented apostles into *cosmos* — an orderly group of men given new inner strength and clarity of purpose.

It is said of our so-called postmodern culture that we have lost our moral compass and have exhausted our feelings and energies. In scriptural terms, we are chaos. Pray to the Spirit, whose divine creativity always produces truth, beauty, goodness, and order — the very qualities our inmost instincts always desire. In our honest moments, we want to be cosmos, an orderly and integrated human being moving with certainty to our eternal destiny and dedicated to love and service during the journey. The Spirit will happily do this for us.

2. FIRE

When the people of Israel marched through the desert wondering where to go, the Spirit came to them as a pillar of fire to lead them through the night of their confusion. In a sense, God is seen in the fire. Without a doubt, God was felt and experienced, for that is the import of the scriptural report. The dynamic Spirit led Israel to salvation and the promised land. The fire provided light for their minds so they could see where to go. It touched their hearts with love so they understood God's motivation in walking with them.

In New Testament times, the people of Israel ritualized their memory of the Pillar of Fire at the Feast of Tabernacles. The night sky was ablaze with festal torches in the Court of the Women on Temple Mount. Four golden candlesticks, each so tall that ladders were needed to reach the tops, were capped with golden bowls of oil with lighted wicks floating in them.

The extravagance of night fire on the eight evenings of Tabernacles was one of the mystic delights of the feast. It probably had the same effect on the celebrants that fireworks have for moderns. Men danced before the Lord, in imitation of David dancing before the Ark, while choirs sang psalms of praise to God the pillar of fire who had walked before their ancestors in the desert.

Onto this splendid stage walked Jesus. In a silent pause between the liturgical psalms and movement, Jesus said, "I am the light of the world. Whoever follows me will not walk in darkness, but will have the light of life" (Jn 8:12). Jesus identified himself with the pillar of fire. The fire is God. In Jesus, God is present before their eyes, just as the fire was to their ancestors. In John's account of the Last Supper, Jesus discoursed at length about his gift of the Spirit to us, a Spirit who would give light to our minds and divine warmth to our souls, a definitive realization of the first pillar of fire for the era of the Church.

Much has been written about the loss of meaning in the twentieth century. Various philosophers have lamented this. Artists have painted the agony of their confusion on hundreds of canvases. People of common sense have seen in the desperateness of the drug culture and the excesses of sexual behavior a faulty and self-destructive response to the decline of meaning.

The image of fire suits the work of the Holy Spirit. The divine spiritual fire offers us wisdom for our intelligence and a soul-satisfying sense of direction for our lives. The Spirit's wisdom is the source of all meaning, the hidden intelligence of God behind the conflicting messages of modernity. As we seek to make sense of our lives, we cannot do better than to beg the holy fire of the Spirit to take hold of our lives and bring us the wisdom to sort out the fragments of contemporary life and create a meaningful whole.

3. Voice

Every Sunday in the Nicene Creed we proclaim that the Spirit "spoke through the prophets." In popular speech we say the prophets were the mouthpieces of God. The Spirit was the Voice and the prophets supplied the words. A prophetic utterance signaled the revelation of the Spirit in human words. Over and over again, the prophets said, "the Word of the Lord came to me." The Spirit came *to* them. Their words came *from* them.

The prophets felt the Spirit of God in their religious ecstasies. (See 1 Samuel 19: 20-24 for an interesting and extended description of the prophetic state.) The Old Testament did not reveal the Spirit as a separate Person in God, but does describe the experience of God in terms of spirit. The prophets, having been touched by God, went forth to preach the Word of the Lord and inspire their listeners to renewed faith and love according to the covenant.

The New Testament presents Jesus, in his prophetic role, as led by the Spirit. "Filled with the holy Spirit, Jesus returned from the Jordan and was led by the Spirit into the desert for forty days . . ." (Lk 4:1). Jesus resisted the temptations in the desert and, like a prophet filled with the Spirit, he embarked on his preaching ministry in Galilee. The Voice of the Spirit was heard in the Word of the Son, a beautiful coordination of the two persons of the Trinity. This truth is enriched by the descriptions of Jesus absorbed in prayer for whole nights on the mountain.

For us the Voice of the Spirit is normally heard in prayer, particularly meditative prayer. In the deep silence of prayer, our hearts become the sounding board of God. This cannot be a casual turn to a time of quiet, but rather a regular, disciplined and daily being still before the Lord. In the Old Testament the Spirit spoke to and through the prophets. Today that same Spirit wishes to speak to us and through us to the world that all peoples may know the loving and saving intentions of God. When we try to share our faith with others, the transforming effect of our sharing is in proportion to the depth of our prayer and the openness of our hearts to the voice of the Spirit.

4. OIL

In Scripture the act of filling someone with God is called an anointing. The visible oil is a sign of an interior blessing. The authority of prophets, kings, and priests was related to their being anointed by God for their office. Prophets were directly anointed by God through a mystical call. This was sometimes visibly evident when the prophet was transfixed in an ecstasy. Kings and priests received visible anointing with oil.

In the New Testament there are several accounts of interior anointing by the Holy Spirit. At Nazareth the Spirit anointed the Virgin Mary. The angel Gabriel told her, "The holy Spirit will come upon you, and the power of the Most High will overshadow you" (Lk 1:35). The Spirit took the humanity that Mary offered and anointed it with the Son of God. This is why Jesus is called the "Christ" which means the oiled, or the anointed one.

When we were baptized the priest anointed us with the oil of the Spirit. Jesus had told Nicodemus, ". . . no one can enter the kingdom of God without being born of water and the Spirit" (Jn 3:5). Our anointing fills us with God. Divine Love wants to be as close to us as we are to ourselves. Just as the Spirit anointed prophets, priests, and kings, so in the Sacrament, the Spirit "oils" us with divine presence and power for our Christian living.

5. DOVE

We all know the story of Noah and the flood. After the rain stopped, Noah sent a dove forth to see if the earth was dry enough for returning to his land. The dove returned with an olive branch, signaling the end of the trial and the restoration of God's friendship with his people. The chaos was gone. The cosmos had reappeared. The breath-Spirit of God had first done this at creation. Now the dove-Spirit of God restores creation. The dove of peace symbolizes the reconciliation of God and people.

The image of the Noah story appears again in the account

of the Baptism of Jesus at the Jordan. The Holy Spirit rested over Jesus in the form of a dove of peace. Why peace? First, because Jesus is the Savior who will restore all people with God. Second, because Christ's identity as Son of God and Messiah is publicly confirmed. The Father tells the world that this is his beloved Son in whom he is well pleased. In his humanity Jesus experienced incomparable peace, symbolized by the dove-Spirit who hovered over him.

In our modern times, the quest for personal identity is crucial. How often the question is raised, "Who am I?" The fragmenting of families and the secularizing of culture have removed the normal ways of knowing our identity. Family and religion were the cornerstones of personal identity for thousands of years. The erosion of these God-given sources of identity has caused confusion and inner, agonizing searching for self.

But the Holy Spirit has not forgotten us. In the chaos of modernity, the Spirit still comes as the "Sign of the Dove" to call us to faith, to baptize us in grace, and to lead us in this way to know who we really are — beloved children of God. Reach for the "Sign of the Dove" and enjoy with Christ the precious gift of self-understanding and the peace which it brings.

This catechesis of the Spirit flows from five biblical images: Breath, Fire, Voice, Oil, and Dove. Scripture and liturgy have many more symbols that help us grasp the interior and powerful action of the Spirit in our lives. When we experience God, we know it is the Spirit making this happen.

RENEW YOUR CONFIRMATION COMMITMENT

At Confirmation the Bishop seals us with the Holy Spirit.

In some ways the reception of the Sacrament is like our personal Pentecost. If we think of the five images of the Spirit mentioned in the catechesis above, we might have a deeper appreciation of what went on at Pentecost and what happened to us at Confirmation.

At Pentecost the Spirit transfigured the men and women in the Upper Room.

(1) The Breath of the Spirit came as a mighty creative "wind" changing the fearful apostles and disciples from timid people lacking confidence to preach and witness Christ to courageous evangelizers fully willing to share the Good News of salvation.

The Spirit also comes to us at our Confirmation, breathing into us the religious backbone we need to stand up for our faith and to live it courageously in our homes and workplaces. Pray this verse: "Breathe on me, breath of God, until my heart is pure. Until with you I have one will to live and to endure."

(2) The Fire of the Spirit rested as a tongue of fire on each member of the Pentecost community. Until that happened they had no sense of direction. They wandered in their desert, not knowing where to go. The fire of the Spirit lit up their minds with the goal of building the Body of Christ and making it a worldwide Church. The fire warmed their hearts to the point that their greatest joy was seeing the new People of God growing from a small seed into a beautiful tree sheltering the world with God's grace.

When we were sealed with the Spirit at Confirmation, the divine fire was offered to our minds to clarify the future of our lives as committed Catholics. The fire reached to our hearts to make us happy when we strengthened our families as members of Christ's Church and reached out to others that they may know the secret wonder of being Catholics. Pray, "Breathe on me, breath of God, fill me with life anew, that I may love the things you love and do what you would do."

(3) At Pentecost the Spirit arose as the Voice which once spoke through the prophets and then spoke fully through Jesus Christ. The very first event that occurred when the community left the Upper Room was the first Christian sermon. Peter stood up before a vast throng and preached the original Gospel, calling the listeners to repent and be baptized in Christ. The Spirit came *to* the apostle. The words came *from* him. The result was the first converts to the Church.

That same Voice of the Spirit was offered to us at Confirmation. The depth of prayer that occurred in the celebration of the sacrament made it possible for the Spirit to speak to us and for us to hear him. One of the important messages preached by the prophets was the need for social justice in the world. Our own day also needs Catholics who are concerned for the poor and unjustly treated. Our prophetic call means we should minister to the poor and the helpless just as Mother Teresa and Dorothy Day did. Pray, "Help us, Lord, to live the faith that we proclaim, that all our thoughts and words and deeds may glorify your holy name."

(4) At Pentecost the Holy Spirit directly anointed the community in the Upper Room, filling them with God. Think of how close oil is to the skin. Then realize that the Spirit is closer to us even than that. Oil evaporates and dries away, but the Spirit is able to stay with our bodies and souls as long as we welcome this divine guest. The God-intoxicated people who streamed out of the Upper Room were so joyful that onlookers thought they were drunk. But Peter said this was not so for it was only nine in the morning. The ecstasy that people saw was caused by the anointing of the Spirit.

The Sacrament of Confirmation fills us with God. The bishop anoints us with oil and says, "Be sealed with the Spirit." Oil feels good. It is smooth and sweet. It symbolizes God's love, the Lord's desire to be absolutely and forever united with the beloved — us. This is a call to a lifelong love relationship with the Spirit. Pray with St. Augustine: "Late have I loved you, O Beauty, ever ancient, ever new, late have I loved you! I have tasted you and now I search for more. You touched me and now I burn for your peace" (*Confessions*, X, 27).

(5) Practically every painting of the Pentecost scene shows a dove at the top streaming rays of light into the members of the community. The Sign of the Dove means the arrival of peace. Until that moment their sense of identity had not been completely clarified. They somewhat knew it in their minds, but it had not taken hold of their full personhoods. They had heard

what Jesus taught them, witnessed his death and resurrection, and even obtained more teachings from the risen Lord. But their identities had not yet crystallized. The descent of the Spirit made all the difference. The dove drove away their doubts and darkness. They knew they were now Temples of the Holy Spirit, Christians called to relive the mysteries of Christ.

Often without strong family life or a clear connection to the Church, we flounder about our human and Christian identities. Confirmation calls the Sign of the Dove to hover over us to clarify the answer to the question, "Who am I?" That is one reason why Confirmation causes so much inner peace for those who celebrate the Sacrament with all their hearts and who renew their commitments made on that beautiful day. Renew your Confirmation promises today and thank the Spirit for these gifts. "Holy Spirit, come confirm us in the truth that Christ makes known. We have faith and understanding through your helping gifts alone."

I hope you have found it helpful to see how the catechesis of the Spirit leads you to celebrate the liturgy of your Confirmation and the renewal of your Confirmation commitment. The Jubilee is a perfect time to do this and to make this a yearly habit on the anniversary of your Confirmation.

MAKE EACH YEAR
A TIME OF LOVE

When all is said and done, the Holy Spirit is the perfect embodiment of love. Should not the Jubilee be a year of love? If I want to be warm I get near the fire. If I want to love, should I not get close to the very source of love? God loved us so much that he sent his Son to save us from sin and give us divine life. Jesus said that he did not come to condemn the world but to save it, to love it away from sin.

The more we love, the more the presence of the Spirit will be experienced. Take the knowledge of God that is in your minds and put it in your hearts. Love the unlovable in others. This is the best way to heal broken lives. The unloved is the unhealed. The loved have the possibility of being made whole.

Mother Teresa attracted the attention of the world by loving those who appeared to be the most unlovable, the seemingly hopeless people dying and neglected in the streets. John F. Kennedy, Jr. visited Mother Teresa in Calcutta several years ago. He noticed how big were the knuckles on her hands, though her body was so small: "I thought of all the pain that had passed through those hands."

She surprised him by immediately asking, "Is that your truck?" "Yes, it is." She said a plane had just arrived with supplies for the sick. "Would you drive me to the airport and help me unload the supplies onto your truck? Don't be surprised. I always ask my visitors to join in helping the poor. I ask and I ask and I ask. I'm shameless, you see."

On the one hand she was tender beyond words to the sick and the poor. Yet for her own sisters, she asked total obedience to the Rule of the community. She did not fear to demand of them the highest surrender to God through the requirements of the Order. She did this in a loving yet unsentimental way. Kennedy wrote that she touched him deeply: "She was the best argument this struggling Catholic has ever met that God truly exists."

When people speak of the sense of the presence of God they may thank the Spirit for this possibility. Jesus promised to be near us through the Spirit. St. Catherine of Siena tells of experiencing a violent temptation. When the storm passed, Jesus appeared to her. She said, "Where were you?" Jesus replied, "I was in your heart." "Impossible," she blurted out, "How could you be within me when I was besieged by such detestable temptations?" Jesus asked her, "Did the thoughts cause you pleasure or pain?" "Terrible pain," said she. "Then," Jesus noted, "You know I was with you. Had I not been there, they would have given you pleasure. It was my presence that made the difference. I defended your heart against temptation. Never have I been closer to you."

Many saints tell us of the Spirit's power which helped them resist evil. Because they know they are loved, they refuse to betray that love. The father of the ancient Christian writer Origen used to bend over the child's cradle and say, "I adore God present in the heart of this little baptized Christian." Sister Elizabeth of the Trinity, a Carmelite known for her outstanding spirituality, once wrote, "Heaven is in the deepest recesses of our souls."

We tend to look for such a treasure everywhere else but in the places closest to us. There is a legend about an Irishman who lived in great poverty in a single room in Galway. One night he dreamt vividly of a treasure beneath a bridge in Dublin. The dream recurred the next two nights. Unable to shake the dream, the man went to Dublin to find the money. He found the exact spot, but there was nothing there.

Sadly, he discussed this with a policeman. The officer laughed and said, "Sure, you should pay no attention to dreams. Why the other night I dreamt about a box of money that was hidden in the walls of a room in Galway." Unwittingly, the policeman described the very room where our friend lived. The officer concluded, "Of course, no sensible man would pay attention to dreams."

Our astonished friend was shocked and absorbed by the policeman's story. He smiled and hastily returned to Galway. He rushed to his room, opened the wall, and found the money that settled him for life. That treasure was with him all along. In order to find it he had to make a long journey. He needed direction to his goal from a stranger, who little realized what he was saying.

We have received the gift of the Holy Spirit to guide us to our goal in life. The treasure of the Spirit is within us. We spend a great deal of energy looking for God and for happiness outside ourselves. The poet T.S. Eliot wrote of such fruitless journeys:

> We shall not cease from exploration.
> And the end of all our exploring

Will be to arrive where we started
And know the place for the first time.
"Little Gidding"

In the Jubilee we will honor the Spirit best by letting the love which he brings flow through our whole selves out to everyone we meet. The Spirit is the love of the Trinity made manifest to us and through us. Love is the greatest proof of God's presence in the world. While we should never abandon the life of the mind — the intellectual pursuits which order the world, give us meaning, and provide for our material needs — we ought also to live from the heart.

Minds stimulate minds indeed, but lasting happiness comes from exchanges of the heart. I read somewhere that the touch of a loving hand reduces blood pressure and stress. The simplicity of love is needed in a world growing increasingly complex. Information overload can be lightened by a smile. The Niagara of data flowing from our computer screens needs the tranquil effect of one person reaching out to another and saying, "I love you." The Holy Spirit of love is present to this surging new world of communications, blessing the human reflection of divine abundance and offering wisdom in the midst of an information assault.

Evangelizers for Christ know that love is the best medicine for healing souls and bringing people to God.

Divine love started the world and redeemed it.

The Jubilee says, "Bring this love to the third millennium."

 Chapter Ten:

Glorified by the Father

Blessed be the God and Father
of our Lord Jesus Christ,
who has blessed us in Christ
with every spiritual blessing. . . .
— Ephesians 1:3

Many celebrated writers today like to portray evil, darkness, and despair. Their novels are like the wild chaos we see in the canvases of modern art. Today's creative writers seem more at home in the nightmares of the subconscious than in the sweet dreams of a good night's rest. The world's sorrows weigh their hearts down. The major problem with their books is the absence of salvation and forgiveness.

Not long ago a young author created just such a short story. He was proud of the misery he so craftily created. A friend of his introduced him to an honored author of the old school, a woman more in touch with perennial values. She asked the young author to read his story to her. Delighted, he read the story.

It concerned the only son of a poor widower who lived in a small two-bedroom home in the Green Mountains of Vermont. One day his son decided to leave home and get a job in New York City. His father's parting words were: "Son, if you ever get in trouble — no matter how dreadful — come home as soon as possible. I am putting this lantern in the window. You will always find it lighted for your return. And I will always be here to welcome you."

Well, the son went off to New York and soon enough found

himself up to his neck in troubles. Wild parties. Liquor. Drugs. All-night binges. Arrested twice. Assaulted in his jail cell. Eventually he was back on the streets, cold and penniless. He had lost his job and all his savings and was so thin his clothes didn't fit him. He finally decided to go home to his father.

He hitched a ride back to Vermont and eagerly used up his waning energies to see his home and his father. But when he came in sight of the old homestead, he stopped. It was night. And the lantern in the window was not burning. End of story. Zip! The author put his pen down on a downbeat ending.

The veteran author looked at him in disbelief and anger. Virtually yelling, she shouted, "Young man, put that lantern back in the window!" She pointed out that stylish writing had gone too far in depicting the traumas and sorrows of life, that it has no room for the happy ending, for the lantern in the window. Even a father's love cannot be counted on.

This literary fashion paints a bleak world without hope.

But that is a very narrow view of reality.

OUR FATHER MADE US. . . . OUR FATHER AWAITS US

How different is Christ's lovely short story of the loving father who forgives his prodigal son. It is a tale of a sinner and a forgiver. In our current culture it seems easier to recall the story of the sinner and harder to remember the message about the forgiver. Why? Because we know it is simpler to sin and difficult to forgive.

Read again this story for the first time in Luke 15:11-32.

Concentrate on the forgiving father, his *attitude* and *behavior*. The father's attitude is fore-giveness, not after-giveness. The father gives ahead of time the loving possibility of reconciliation. He does not require groveling apologies. He has no wish to humble his son. It was not a case of, "Apologize, then I will forgive you." No, it was a matter of, "I always have a forgiving heart toward you. No discussions needed. Come back to me. You are always welcome in my heart and home."

That is the father's attitude.

What is the father's behavior?

First, *he hugs his son.* In fact he does it with such warmth and affection, that he smothers any attempt of his son to blurt out his planned apologies, his prepared repentance speech. Dr. Blanton, in his book *The Magic of Touch*, says that he once heard a family court judge say that of all the hundreds of juvenile offenders and their parents who came before him, he never saw a parent put a protective arm around a youngster's shoulder. But the father in Christ's story cannot wait to embrace his beloved son.

Second, *he puts shoes on his son's feet.* In biblical times, free people wore shoes. Slaves went barefoot. This was true in early slave times in America. No wonder the blacks sang at Church, "All God's Children Gonna Wear Shoes." The father liberates his son from the slavery of sin and gives him the freedom of the house and equal membership in the family.

Third, *he puts a ring on his finger.* Almost certainly this was a ring with a family seal on it. This means he gave his son the right to seal papers and letters that dealt with important transactions in family affairs, something like being a co-signer in a checking account. He gave his son a sign of trust. The Fathers of the Church saw here a memory of what happened to Joseph of Eygpt when the Pharaoh said to him, " 'You shall be in charge of my palace. . . .' With that he took off his signet ring and put it on Joseph's finger" (Gen 41:40, 42).

In this lovely parable, Jesus is describing God our Father. Jesus tells us how full of love and forgiveness is the Father. St. John repeats Christ's characterization of the Father, "God is love" (1 Jn 4:8). "For God so loved the world that he gave his only Son. . ." (Jn 3:16).

Jesus saved us. The Holy Spirit sanctifies us. The Father waits for us to come to him so he can glorify us in eternal life.

This is the Trinitarian horizon for our Jubilee celebration. We have reflected on Jesus as our Savior and the Spirit as the one who leads us on the journey of holiness. This journey has a goal; it is a passage to the Father who has a heart brimming with love for us and "arms" so big he can embrace every human being who hungers for his love.

FIVE PATHS TO OUR FATHER OF THE JUBILEE

Pope John Paul II connects five teachings with our appreciation of our Father of the Jubilee:

1. Conversion of Lifestyle
2. Renewal of the Sacrament of Reconciliation
3. Creation of a Civilization of Love
4. Preferential Option for the Poor
5. Serious Dialogue with Non-Christian Religions

Let us look briefly at each teaching which is also a path on our journey to our Father.

(1) *Convert Your Lifestyle.* Jubilees and anniversaries are ideal times to evaluate our lives. Where have we been? Where are we now? Where do we expect to go? The Jubilee 2000 invites us to conduct a comprehensive examination of conscience. It has been said that the unexamined life is not worth living. Therefore, the examined life has a better chance to get a new start that is worth living.

Expectation affects performance. The lower my goals, the less I will achieve. The higher my goals, the greater the possibility of my fulfillment.

There was a school experiment conducted some years ago in which one teacher was given bright students, but told they had low IQs. The result was they performed far below their potential. Another teacher was given slow students but told they had very high IQs. All her students performed far above their imagined potential. The difference was in the expectation that affected their performance.

People in a marathon race keep their eyes on the gold medal. This makes them practice harder and sacrifice all other interests so they can win the gold. Maybe the runner will only get a silver medal, but had the racer set the bronze medal as the goal, he or she may finish far behind the winners. Keep raising the expectation and the achievement will be more satisfactory.

This psychology underlies the call to holiness which demands the process of conversion of lifestyle. It does not help to say, "Oh, I can't be holy. That's for saints. I'll settle for less." But why? Why not want to be the best? Of course in spiritual matters this will always involve the grace of the Holy Spirit to guide us and strengthen us with divine powers for the journey. Now the Spirit never tells us to pick a low goal.

Each of us has been given a secret gift from God. This grace is both for our salvation and our holiness. It is a light we are meant to shine in the world. Every one of us is a star. We may differ from others in the kind and intensity of glory we are meant to shine, but glow we should so that our neighborhood will be filled with God's light. This is the gold medal that should motivate us to enter on the process of conversion in the Jubilee 2000.

(2) *Renew the Sacrament of Reconciliation*. It's no secret that the Confession lines have grown shorter in the last thirty years. But people have kept on sinning. For whatever reason, they have found other ways to deal with their consciences. Yet the Church still has confessionals, whether for face-to-face encounters or the private approach.

I was pleasantly surprised during a visit to St. Patrick's Cathedral not long ago. The sign announced Confessions before all the Masses on weekdays, as well as an hour set aside every day at noon. I noticed that several confessionals were open and the lines were long. Confession was alive and well. I have heard that some parishes are offering the Sacrament of Reconciliation at 5 p.m. on weekdays in the hopes that parishioners will stop by on their way home from work. The first results have been impressive, with a great number of people happy to take advantage of this convenient time to have their hearts renewed and their sins cleansed away by the power of Christ through the mediation of the priest in the sacrament.

Some people have hurtful memories of Confession, recalling an emphasis on the sins and God as a so-called angry judge. There needed to be a balanced response which characterized Confession as a positive experience of grace given to us by a loving Father who rejoices to welcome us home to his friendship. In many cases there was what I would call a reaction rather than a response. A reaction is a thoughtless, knee-jerk event. In some this resulted in a convenient denial of sinfulness. In others it created a God of compassion who was so nice and kind, he never noticed we had any sins. This is a dishonest compassion, a love separated from truth.

I think a turnaround has occurred. The tide is turning toward a sensible realism about our moral condition and a balanced understanding of God as a loving, compassionate judge who wants us to confess our sins and be reconciled to him, to the Church, and to ourselves. The renewal of the Sacrament of Reconciliation in Jubilee 2000 is a most valued goal for us all.

(3) *Create a Civilization of Love.* It is no secret that our culture has been secularized far beyond what anybody ever expected. The new technology is breathtaking and challenging and should benefit humanity in new and striking ways. But at the same time the moral compass of this new world is raging out of control. We all know the ravages of abortion. But now there is the specter of euthanasia, whose doctor-assisted suicide is but the camel's nose in the tent.

How quickly we are descending the slippery slope. An MIT professor has taken to the pages of the *New York Times* to defend infanticide. He argued that babies are not yet equipped with values or the capacity to make decisions. Therefore, they are disposable, just as much as fetuses, and, we might, add the old, the sick, and those with disabilities.

The secular response to the AIDS epidemic has virtually nothing to do with the moral order or the behavior of the people who cause AIDS. The sexual revolution continues on its merry — or should we say tragic — way. Too many young people grow up without hearing about moral standards, whether about sex or other issues for that matter.

Pope John Paul calls this a "crisis of civilization." He urges us to make Jubilee 2000 a time to launch a major effort to create a civilization of love. This is a love practiced in truth. It is a love connected to the life of the theological virtues of faith, hope, and love and the cardinal virtues of prudence, justice, temperance, and courage. It is a love that should find concrete expression in obedience to the Ten Commandments.

This is a love that goes far beyond the sentimental vision of love promoted in popular entertainment. The poets infuse love with iron when they say that love is as strong as death, even stronger, for love conquers all (*Amor vincit omnia*). There can be no civilization of love without religious faith and moral values and the life of the virtues. Actually there can be no civilization at all without these elements.

There is a coarseness about our civilization in crisis. Its tawdry face — on our TV screens, in our movie houses, our novels and paintings, on the live stage, and in the breakdown of civility in everyday treatment of one another — depresses us.

Yet despite this, the culture is peopled with huge numbers of good people, determined to conserve humanity and faith in God. A community of faith and love does exist. We need to shine our light of Christ and share our faith in a loving Father to begin a process of re-civilizing our culture and providing it with the religious and moral basis that will save it from itself.

(4) *Have a Preferential Option for the Poor*. All the papal encyclicals from Leo XIII to John Paul II give us the Church's social teachings which claim that the goods of the earth are a gift from God meant for the good of every human being. This is especially true for the widow, the orphan, the stranger, and the hundreds of millions of dirt-poor people in every country around the world.

The poor need a voice. Catholics can give them this voice and work to create a world of justice and peace, from the barrios of Latin American to the urban ghettoes and mountain towns in Appalachia in the United States. The neediest always require our compassion and positive attention. One of Christ's first sermons dealt with our responsibility to help the poor (see Luke 4:16-21).

Jesus was born of poor people among the poor of a poverty-laden colony of the Roman Empire. Jesus, the King of Kings, knew what it was like to be poor. He always had a preferential option for the poor. Mother Teresa awoke a whole world to her mission to the poorest of the poor. St. Francis said his spouse was Lady Poverty, not because he wanted everyone to be poor, but because he was then free to help the poor and call others to assist them as well.

Christ has called the Church to be a powerful advocate for the poor, to alleviate the symptoms of their poverty and to change unjust social structures that keep them poor. One of the original purposes of a biblical Jubilee was freedom and assistance for the poor and oppressed. Jubilee 2000 is the perfect opportunity for us to identify with the Church's preferential option for the poor.

(5) *Dialogue with Non-Christian Religions.* The Church uses the expression "interreligious dialogue" to characterize her conversations with non-Christian religions while calling dialogue with other Christian faiths "ecumenism." Because of the closeness of Judaism to Christianity due to its being the people of the first covenant, our dialogue has a unique quality. We share a spiritual richness and heritage of faith that benefits from the partriarchs, prophets, and wisdom writers.

Since the tragedy of the Holocaust there has been a special effort by the Church to eliminate anything within the community of faith which would foster anti-semitism. Since so many Catholic shrines celebrate the mysteries of Christ in the Holy Land (especially in Jerusalem), the Vatican and the Israeli government are engaging in continuing dialogue about the integrity and protection of these holy places.

Another priority for dialogue is with the third great monotheistic religion, Islam. The Muslims honor Jesus as a prophet and have a special affection for Christ's mother Mary who is mentioned many times in the Koran. The sheer sweep and size of Islam from Morocco across the belt of the world to Indonesia is indicative of the powerful presence of Muslims in the world. Their growing presence in Western Europe and in the United States is another reason for our need to understand them and to help them appreciate our faith.

We should eliminate whatever tensions our differences could create and share our mutual spiritual traditions. They have the "seeds of the Word." This is how the Vatican Council referred to what may be considered the authentic work of God in Islam and other world religions such as Hinduism and Buddhism, especially in the area of prayer and meditation.

Pope John Paul II envisions Jubilee meetings with Jews and Muslims. "Attention is being given to arranging historic meetings in places of exceptional symbolic importance like Bethlehem, Jerusalem, and Mount Sinai as a means of furthering dialogue with Jews and the followers of Islam, and to arranging similar meetings elsewhere with the leaders of the great world religions. However, care will always have to be taken not to cause harmful misunderstandings, avoiding the risk of syncretism and of a facile, deceptive irenicism" ("The Coming Third Millennium," 53).

The above five steps form a vigorous challenge for us in Jubilee 2000 for our journey to our Father. Conversion of lifestyle means we want to set the highest expectations for ourselves because that leads to the best performance with God the Father's help. The renewal of the Sacrament of Reconciliation reasserts the meaning of Christ's redemption from sins and places us in an honest and forthright position regarding our conscience and moral life. We are like the Prodigal Son welcomed home by an all-loving Father. The support for a civilization of love will profit a culture lost in anxiety and despair because it has abandoned contact with our heavenly Father. The preferential option for the poor fully implements the

Father's will that his creation is for everyone's benefit, not just the rich and powerful. God is the Father of all the world's peoples and the members of all the religions on earth. A generous involvement in interreligious dialogue with the members of world religions is a process that, with the Holy Spirit's help, may one day lead to their finding the joy and peace of Jesus Christ and his salvation.

CONCLUDING THOUGHTS

Our reflection on the millennium has taken us in two directions. In Part One of this book, I reviewed with you the millennium as the "End of the World." I took up themes about the rapture, the antichrist, the tribulations, Armageddon, the Second Coming, and the medieval predictions of Joachim of Fiore. I hope I have been reasonably fair to the positions of current millenarians including the fact that they have various schools of thought about the end of time.

I have tried in each instance to give the Catholic response to the millenarian teachings, especially contrasting their "four last things" with the way Catholics look at these signs of the end. I have noted that modern millenarians take more seriously than most Christians the doctrine of the Second Coming. Their interest in this part of divine revelation gives them their current enthusiasm and dynamism.

All Christians could benefit from a serious look at the doctrine of the Second Coming. Catholics are confronted with it every year on the thirty-third Sunday of Ordinary Time, when one of the Last Judgment Gospels is read. Catholics also encounter Second Coming teachings throughout Advent when the biblical texts about the first coming of Jesus at Bethlehem also have a resonance with Christ's final coming in glory.

At the same time, millenarians might profit from Catholic reserve about dating the Second Coming and Catholic reticence about applying biblical prophecy literally to geopolitical events in the modern world. Christ's Second Coming will happen, but it is a mystery of faith, a "mystery" in the sense that it is an event hidden in God's plans as to when and how it will happen. Whereof man cannot speak, thereof let him be silent. A prudent silence is the best response to dates and methods of Christ's final coming in glory.

In Part Two of this book, I shared with you a vision of the millennium as a Great Jubilee celebrating the Redemption. Christ has saved us from our sins. The Spirit is sanctifying us with an abundance of graces. The Father awaits us in the future to glorify us in eternal life. All this is ours, if our faith opens our hearts to these wonderful mysteries of God's love.

Chapter eight on Jesus recovers the plan of the Father who loved the world so much that he sent Jesus to save us. Jesus does not come to condemn the world, but to love its sins away. I contrast the world of Christ's time with its basic religious outlook to the world of today with its resolutely secular inclination. Our capacity to share Jesus with the world today will be enhanced when we fully appreciate the secularity of the culture we hope to evangelize. It can be done.

The Roman Empire must have looked frightening and overwhelming to the first Christian missionaries, yet within less than three centuries, Christianity became the official religion of the empire. Secularity may discourage us with its pervasiveness and seeming power, but we can share Christ with today's "powers that be," for they need the absolute love and hope that the old Romans hungered for. Underneath all culture beats the same human heart with the same needs. Let Christ love and save the world through us.

Our Jubilee will draw our attention to the sanctifying work of the Holy Spirit. I offered you a series of biblical images as a catechesis of the activity of the Spirit seen in Scripture as: Breath, Fire, Voice, Oil, and Dove. These "pictures" of the Spirit come together at Pentecost when the revelation of the Spirit occurs. Each of us experiences the presence of the Spirit at our Baptisms and Confirmations. Throughout our lives the Spirit leads us through the process of sanctification, if we are open to his desire to help us.

The Holy Spirit provides us with an experience of the living God. When we stay in touch with the Spirit we have the potential to be dynamic Catholics, gladly sharing our faith with others as evangelists for Christ.

Jubilee 2000 will also put us in touch with our heavenly Father, who awaits us and wants to glorify us in eternal life. Our Father calls us to a conversion of our lifestyle, a renewed commitment to the Sacrament of Reconciliation, a desire to create a civilization of love, a preferential option for the poor, and an interest in dialogue with world religions.

MARY AND THE MILLENNIUM

Pope John Paul II always turns our attention to our Blessed Mother at the conclusion of every pastoral letter he writes. Mary is an essential part of our millennial celebration. As Mother of Christ, she draws us to her beloved Son. As Mother of the Church, Mary asks us to love the Church and be courageous in witnessing what the Church asks us to do in the world. The Church is the Body of Christ. It extends the presence and action of Christ in history.

Mary is our ideal example of what a disciple of Jesus should be. Her obedience to the call of God at the Annunciation, when she joyfully said she wanted to do the Father's will, is a model for our own interior attitude to the Father's loving desires for us. Every day we should also say to God, "Whatever you want, Lord. Be it done unto me according to your will."

Mary's last words in the Bible referred to Jesus. "Do whatever he tells you" (Jn 2:5). Mary is always saying that to us. She wants us to listen to Jesus as his word comes to us interiorly through the Spirit and externally through the Church and the circumstances of our lives. This is a loving and urgent invitation that will bring us joy and fulfillment and make the world a better place.

In conclusion I quote John Paul:

> I entrust the Church to the maternal interces-
> sion of Mary, Mother of the Redeemer. She,
> the Mother of Fairest Love, will be for Chris-
> tians on the way to the Great Jubilee of the
> Third Millennium, the Star which guides their
> steps to the Lord (Pope John Paul II, "The
> ComingThird Millennium," 59).

INDEX

A Planet to Heal, 22
Abraham, 26, 106
Adams, Fred, 20
Adler, Mortimer, 105
Adrian VI, 121
Age of the Father, 68
Age of the Son, 68
Age of the Spirit, 68-71, 75, 79
AIDS, 140
Allah, 25
Antichrist, 10, 31-41, 45-46, 50, 51, 52, 53, 60, 62-63, 66, 82, 144
Antiochus IV, 32, 34-37, 39, 49
Apocalypse, 13, 24-25, 28, 32, 34, 37, 39, 41, 64, 68, 71, 82, 85, 86, 87
Aquinas, Thomas, St., 68-69, 105
Armageddon, 33, 42, 46, 85-86, 144
Arrupe, Pedro, 22
Ascension, 83
Astronomers, 20-21
Atomic Clock, 22
Augustine, St., 10, 19, 67, 70-74, 79, 87, 107, 130

Babylonians, 34, 36, 58
Baldwin, Robert, 45
Baptism, 12, 87, 108, 128
Barnicle, Mike, 110

Bernard, St., 89
Black Plague, 40
Blessed Mother, 48, 108, 146
Book of Daniel, 10, 32, 35, 36, 55-57
Book of Ezekiel, 35
Book of Revelation, 25, 28, 39, 79, 82
Breath, 39, 121, 123, 128, 129, 145

Catechism of the Catholic Church, 106
Catherine of Siena, St., 97, 132
Catholics, 10-11, 52, 84, 88, 93, 97, 106-107, 121-122,
    129-130, 141, 144, 146
China, 25, 33, 41, 46
Christ, 10 *et passim*
Church, 9 *et passim*
City of God, 70-71, 74
*The Clash of Civilizations and the Remaking of the
    World Order*, 25
The Clowns of God, 17
Cold War, 22-23, 33
Communism, 25, 40, 81
Confirmation, 12, 122, 128-131
The cornerstone, 59
Cosby, Bill, 26
Crossing the Threshold of Hope, 13

Dallas Theological Seminary, 31
Darby, John Nelson, 45

Dark Era, 21
Death, 18-19, 21, 62, 69, 82, 83, 84, 89-92, 107, 114, 130, 141
Decline and Fall of the Roman Empire, 24
Degenerate Era, 21
Decartes, 112-113
Dobson, Ed, 62
Dove, 27, 127-128, 130-131, 145

Eliot, T.S., 133
The End of the World: A Catholic View, 45
European Common Market, 32, 36
Ezekiel, 74-79, 85

The Fall, 20, 31, 38, 46, 59
Father Elijah, 40
Fire, 22, 36, 38-39, 46, 55, 77, 86, 89, 110, 121, 124-125, 128-129, 131, 145
Four beasts, 36, 59-60

Generation X, 117
Gog, 35-36, 39, 49
Great apostasy, 39
Greek Empire, 58-59
Greeks, 36
Gregory XI, Pope, 97

Heaven, 13, 19, 38, 43, 45-46, 47-48, 68, 70, 82, 83, 91-93, 122, 133
Hell, 46, 82, 87, 89, 92-93
Hickey, Daniel, 109-110
Hickey, Father Jim, 109-110
Hispanics, 25
Hitler, 40
Holy Spirit, 12 *et passim*
Hopkins, Gerald Manley, 81
Hymn to the Word Incarnate, 116

Illig, Father Alvin, 118
Isaiah, 65, 101-102
Islam, 25, 142-143

Japan, 25
Jesus, 11 *et passim*
Jewish State, 31
Jewish Theological Seminary, 9
Jews, Jewish, Judaism, 31-32, 34-35, 41-42, 45, 47, 61, 68, 75-79, 121, 142, 143
Joachim of Fiore, 7, 10, 67, 70, 79, 144
Joan of Arc, 107
John, St., 12, 25, 31, 33, 79, 82, 86, 113-114, 124-125, 137
John's Gospel, 17, 111, 124
John Paul II, Pope, 9, 11, 13, 23, 98, 103, 108, 110, 117-118, 120, 138, 141, 143, 146-147

Jubilee, 9-13, 95, 97-101, 102, 104, 131, 134, 137-143, 145-147
Jubilee 2000, 11, 104, 107-108, 122, 138-143, 146
Judas Maccabeus, 34, 92
Judgment, *see also* Last Judgment, 27, 33, 60, 90, 91

Kennedy, John F. Jr., 132
King Nebuchadnezzar, 57

Last Judgment, 10, 18, 22, 82, 85, 87, 89, 103, 144
The Late Great Planet Earth, 31
Little horn, 36
Loughlin, Greg, 20
Lindsey, Hal, 31

MAD (Mutually Assured Destruction), 23
Madeline Jacobs, 20
Mandela, Nelson, 29
Mark of the beast, 45
Martin, Malachi, 40
Martini, Cardinal Carlo Maria, 13
Medes, 36, 58-59
Millenarians, 9-11, 45, 72, 78, 83-88, 93, 144
Millennialists, 31, 36, 41, 43-44, 46, 51-52, 60-63, 65
Millennium, 9-10, 11-12, 13-14, 17, 18, 31, 37, 45-46, 69-70, 74-75, 77, 81-82, 86, 87, 88, 90, 97, 98, 99, 103, 108, 110, 113, 116, 118-119, 122, 134, 143-147

Miller, William, 55, 57
Montanus, 86-87
Monte Cassino, 17-18
Mother Teresa, 130, 132, 142

Nazism, 40
The Name of the Rose, 13
Nero, 37, 40
New Testament, 4, 10-11, 50, 52, 59, 62, 68, 91, 113, 116, 123-124, 126-127
Nicene Creed, 10, 17-18, 53, 63, 88, 105, 123, 125
Noah, 26-29, 127
Noah Precedent, 26, 29

O'Brien, Michael, 40
Oil, 25, 124, 127, 128, 130, 145
Old Testament, 34, 49, 68, 99, 100, 116, 126
Origen, 87, 133

Parable of the Dry Bones, 77
Paraclete, 114
Parousia, 45, 49-53, 64, 84
Paul, St., 39, 43-44, 46-53, 59, 62, 83-84, 88, 107
Persians, 34-36, 58-59
Peter, St., 59, 92, 118, 121-122, 129, 130
Pharisees, 35

Prayer of Commendation, 90
Purgatory, 92, 93

Rapture, 10, 43-46, 50-53, 82-84, 86, 88, 144
Roman Empire, 24, 37, 58-60, 63, 65, 142, 145
Russia, 23, 32, 41
Sabbath, 9
Sacrament of Reconciliation, 13, 87, 104, 114-115,
    138-140, 143, 146
Scofield Reference Bible, 44
Scripture, 10, 20, 28, 33, 35, 37, 40, 44, 47, 52, 55, 56,
    57, 63, 64, 72, 79, 82, 92, 100, 102, 106, 108, 118,
    119, 123, 127, 128, 145
Second Coming, 10-11, 17, 34, 39, 45, 47-50, 61, 63,
    82, 83, 84, 85, 86, 87, 88, 89, 91, 93, 103, 144
Second Temple, 31-32
Seventy weeks of years, 55, 60-66
Snow, Samuel, 57
Stalin, Joseph, 40

Tertio Adveniente Millennio, 98
Thessalonians, 33, 39, 43-44, 46-48, 50, 53, 57, 83-84,
    88
Third millennium, 10-11, 14, 97, 98, 103, 108, 116,
    118, 119, 122, 134, 143, 147
Thirty-third Sunday of Ordinary Time, 10, 144
Thousand-year reign, 11, 45, 82, 85-86
Timothy, 47

Tribulations, 25, 29, 32, 46, 53, 70, 71, 82, 85-86, 144
Trinity, 48, 68, 83, 88, 91, 123, 126, 134
Tuchman, Barbara, 81, 97

Vietnam, 25
Voice, 43, 75, 125-126, 128-129, 141, 145

Windswept House, 40
World War III, 25
World Youth Day, 117

Year 2000, 10-11, 18, 24-25, 31, 42, 98-99, 103, 110

Our Sunday Visitor...
Your Source for Discovering the Riches of the Catholic Faith

Our Sunday Visitor has an extensive line of materials for young children, teens, and adults. Our books, Bibles, booklets, CD-ROMs, audios, and videos are available in bookstores worldwide.

To receive a FREE full-line catalog or for more information, call **Our Sunday Visitor** at **1-800-348-2440**. Or write, **Our Sunday Visitor** / 200 Noll Plaza / Huntington, IN 46750.

Please send me: __ A catalog
Please send me materials on:
    __ Apologetics and catechetics   __ Reference works
    __ Prayer books   __ Heritage and the saints
    __ The family   __ The parish

Name_____

Address_____Apt._____

City_____State___Zip_____

Telephone (   )_____

A89BBABP

Please send a friend: __ A catalog
Please send a friend materials on:
    __ Apologetics and catechetics   __ Reference works
    __ Prayer books   __ Heritage and the saints
    __ The family   __ The parish

Name_____

Address_____Apt._____

City_____State___Zip_____

Telephone (   )_____

A89BBABP

Our Sunday Visitor
200 Noll Plaza
Huntington, IN 46750
1-800-348-2440
OSVSALES@AOL.COM

Your Source for Discovering the Riches of the Catholic Faith